The Boxer

Sheila Webster Boneham, Ph.D.

The Boxer

Project Team
Editor: Stephanie Fornino
Copy Editor: Carl Schutt
Design: Lundquist Design
Series Design: Mada Design
Series Originator: Dominique De Vito

T.F.H. Publications
President/CEO: Glen S. Axelrod
Executive Vice President: Mark E. Johnson
Publisher: Christopher T. Reggio
Production Manager: Kathy Bontz

T.F.H. Publications, Inc.
One TFH Plaza
Third and Union Avenues
Neptune City, NJ 07753

Library of Congress Cataloging-in-Publication Data Boneham, Sheila Webster, 1952- The boxer / Sheila Webster Boneham.
p. cm.
ISBN 0-7938-3630-1 (alk. paper)
1.   Boxer (Dog breed) I. Title.
SF429.B75B59 2005
636.73—dc22
2005009887

The Leader In Responsible Animal Care For Over 50 Years!™
www.tfhpublications.com

TABLE OF CONTENTS

1
HISTORY
O F T H E B O X E R

For more than three quarters of a century, the handsome, personable Boxer has held his own in the hearts of dog lovers in the US and abroad. The Boxer's expressive, intelligent face, athletic body, and companionable personality attract many admirers, and for good reason. In the right sort of home, this is truly a dog for all seasons. Companion, teammate, defender, friend—the Boxer can be all of these and more.

Like all breeds, the Boxer we know today was developed from dogs who were bred for specific purposes, and the genes that made his ancestors successful are still part of the modern Boxer. If you're thinking of owning a Boxer, you may find that some knowledge of the breed's history will make it easier to understand the characteristics of the modern Boxer, which I'll discuss in more detail in Chapter 2.

EARLY ANCESTORS OF THE BOXER

The Boxer's origins lie in the distant mists of the ancient Near East and Mediterranean, where some 4,000 years ago, the Assyrians and others began to use large, powerful dogs as weapons of war. The name "Molossian," for the city of Molossus in what is now Albania, was eventually applied to these dogs, whose popularity spread across Europe. Selective breeding for different purposes led to the development of different types of Molossians. In England, a larger dog, ancestor to the modern Mastiff, was created. In Germany, descendants of the Molossians became the Bullenbeisser, who was popular as a hunting dog. His undershot bite enabled him to breathe while hanging on to such game as bears and boars.

Serious, selective breeding of dogs wasn't practiced in Germany until the late nineteenth century, although different types of dogs did evolve as people selected individual animals suited to specific purposes. Animal fighting was a popular sport in medieval England and Germany, and the term "Dogge" was used to denote any of a range of strong, muscular, short-haired dogs with large heads, powerful muzzles, strong teeth, and abundant courage and tenacity. Eventually, these "Doggen" evolved into three types from which modern breeds developed. One of these three was the heavy Bullenbeisser, who eventually became the Mastiff. The Bullenbeisser was also crossed with Wolfhounds and Deerhounds to create the large hunting dog we know as the Great Dane, and a smaller version of the heavy Bullenbeisser became the Boxer and the Bulldog. Doggen and Bullenbeisser were prized by hunters because the dogs attacked game from behind and were therefore less prone to injury than other hunting dogs who attacked head-on. Their powerful jaws also enabled them to hang on to game until the hunter arrived, and so deliberate breeding advanced.

A smaller Bullenbeisser who figures directly in the modern Boxer's ancestry was developed in northeastern Belgium. These "Brabanter Bullenbeissers" had their ears cropped and tails docked, a practice continued in Germany. When the large feudal holdings of German nobility were broken up after the Napoleonic wars, the Bullenbeissers who had once lived and hunted bear and wild boar in packs left behind their lives on estates to become the companions and guardians of farmers and tradesmen. Their intelligence, tractability, and versatility kept them alive when many other breeds were disappearing during the social upheavals of the times.

THE MODERN BOXER IN GERMANY

The Boxer began his development as a distinct breed around Munich, Germany, beginning in the late 1800s, and the first Boxer club was formed in Munich in 1895. Dog people just seem to be competitors at heart, so naturally the first Boxer show was held as soon as possible. The first breed standard for the Boxer was also set down, and it still influences contemporary Boxer standards. A stud book, a record of all dogs in the breed who produce offspring, was established with the registration of MЯhlbauer's Flocki in 1904, a dog whose sire was a white Bulldog known as Dr. Toneissen's Tom and whose dam was a bitch known as Alt's Shecken.

Systematic development of the modern Boxer commenced when Alt's Flora, a brindle bitch, was imported to Germany from France by George Alt and bred to a local dog whose name is lost to us, but whose genetic contribution remains with Boxers today. That cross produced Lechner's Box, a fawn and white male. He was bred back to Flora and produced two puppies. One was Alt's Shecken, dam of the first stud-book registrant. The other was Alt's Flora II.

Flora II was bred to her sire, Box, and produced Maier's

Lord, who went on to become the first Boxer sire of renown. Maier's Lord was bred to Maier's Flora, a bitch of unknown parentage, producing Piccolo von Angertor. He in turn was bred to Champion Blanka von Angertor, who was from a second breeding of Schecken and Dr Toneissen's Tom. That cross produced Meta von der Passage, a very influential dam. Her offspring, sired by Flock St. Salvator and Wotan, are found in all modern Boxer pedigrees. Flock St. Salvator is particularly important for American Boxer lovers. He sired Meta's son, Hugo von Pfalzgau, who was the great-grandsire of Rolf von Vogelsberg. Rolf in turn was the foundation sire of the German vom Dom line of Boxers, which is at the heart of most American Boxer lines.

The Boxer began its development as a distinct breed in Germany.

BOXERS IN THE UNITED STATES

The first Boxers set foot in America in 1904, with a few more arriving after World War I. Over the next 30 years, only 71 Boxers were registered in the US, but by 1938 the number had jumped to 724, and the Boxer assumed his place as one

Inbreeding

It's important to understand that inbreeding is necessary to establish any breed, and the Boxer is no exception. Inbreeding, or crossing of close relatives with desirable genetic traits, is the only way to "set type"—that is, to ensure that the genetic makeup of future generations is consistent, so that when you breed one individual to another, the offspring will have the traits you expect and want. Although excessive inbreeding over too many generations can lead to a concentration of problem traits, careful inbreeding and line-breeding, a form of inbreeding between more distant relatives, are what create and preserve the breeds we know and love.

of America's best-loved breeds, both as a family companion and in the show ring. The history of the Boxer in the US was shaped in large part by the contributions of German breeders Friederun Stockmann, her husband Philip, and the dogs of their vom Dom kennel.

Stockmann began her long involvement in Boxers when, at about 20 years of age, she purchased Rolf von Vogelsberg. Rolf, who was about three years old at that time, epitomized the working show dog, earning the German title of "Sieger" (Grand Victor at a Sieger, or winners' show) multiple times and serving with Philip Stockmann on the front lines in World War I. Rolf was also an influential sire in the early development of the breed.

Rolf's son, Dampf vom Dom, who was whelped September 28, 1912, became Stockmann's first homebred champion. He was sold to Governor and Mrs. Lehman of New York, and in 1915 became the first Boxer to finish an AKC championship. Because there were few bitches in the US at that time, Dampf made no significant contribution to the gene pool, but he did awaken an interest in the breed.

Several of Rolf's other descendants did, however, become major sires of the German Boxer bloodlines, including, in direct descent from Rolf: Champion Rolf Walhall, Champion Moritz von Goldrain, Champion Caesar von Deutenkofen, and Champion Buko von Biederstein. In 1925, Buko sired a dog named Ivein vom Dom, who became the foundation for the post-WWI rebuilding of the vom Dom line of Boxers. Ivein carried Rolf von Vogelsberg's genes on both sides. His dam, Zwibel, was Rolf's granddaughter, and his sire, Buko von Biederstein, was Rolf's great-great-grandson. Iwein's son, Sigurd von Dam of Barmere, became a major figure in both German and American Boxers.

Sigurd, who was whelped by the Stockmanns in 1929, spent his early years in Germany, where his abilities as a show dog and as a sire equaled those of his famous forebear, Rolf von Vogelsberg. In May 1934, Sigurd was imported by Charles Ludwig and then sold to the Barmere Kennels in Van Nuys, California. In 1935, he won Best of Breed at the prestigious Westminster Kennel Club dog show. His American show record included 2 Best in Show, 54 Best of Breed, and 43 Group wins. (Boxers were at that time shown in the Non-sporting Group.) Sigurd was the leading Boxer sire of 1936 and second to his own grandsons in 1939 and 1940. His offspring included 16 American-bred and 10 imported champions. He died at 13 years of age, on March 3, 1942.

Ten of Sigurd's German-born sons and daughters were eventually brought to the US, where they earned championships and produced champion pups. All told, 55 of Sigurd's offspring earned American championships or produced champions. Three of Sigurd's imported

The first Boxers set foot in America in the early 1900s.

grandsons—Utz vom Dom, Lustig vom Dom, and Dorian von Marienhof—were particularly influential in the development of the Boxer in the US.

Champion Lustig vom Dom, who became International Champion Lustig vom Dom of Tulgey Woods, was purchased at a time when the Stockmanns needed the impressive price offered for him. Lustig, who was renowned for his outstanding head and expression, earned his American championship like a whirlwind in a single week with one Best in Show, two Group Firsts, and one Group Fourth (first and fourth place, respectively, in the Group competition, which at that time was the Non-sporting Group). He was the sire of 41 American-bred and imported Boxers who became American champions, and 25 additional American-bred and imported dogs used for breeding in the US. Lustig died on June 14, 1945.

Champion Utz vom Dom, whelped in Germany on April 18, 1936, was Lustig's full brother. At the age of three, he was imported by John Wagner for his famous Mazelaine Kennels, and he went on to become an American champion and to win the Working Group at Westminster in 1940. By the end of 1947, Utz had sired 35 champions and 16 additional dogs used for breeding. He died in 1945, two months before Lustig.

International Champion Dorian von Marienhof of Mazelaine, who was whelped in April 1933, was the last of the four American foundation sires imported from Germany. His sire was International Champion Xerxes vom Dom, a full brother to Zorn vom Dom, who sired Lustig and Utz. Dorian won Best of Breed at Westminster in 1936 and became the first Boxer to win the Working Group there a year later. Throughout his show career, Dorian was undefeated in his breed and garnered 22 Best in Show wins. Dorian, who was a large brindle dog, sired 39 imported and American-bred champions, as well as another 8 dogs who produced champions.

The American Boxer Club and the Breed Standard

The American Boxer Club (ABC), formed in 1935, was one of many AKC affiliate breed clubs formed in that decade. Seventeen founding members met in New York City on February 16th, applied formally for membership in the American Kennel Club on March 21st, and were approved on May 14th. The club then petitioned the AKC to move the Boxer from the Non-sporting to the Working Group, which was approved the same year.

By 1936, membership in the ABC had doubled to 35, and the same number of Boxers competed in the club's first specialty show on June 6, 1936 in Porchester, New York. Champion Corso v. Uracher Wasserfall se Sumbula, an import, was Best of Breed that year and the following year.

A great deal of controversy surrounded the breed standard at that time. The first official standard adopted by the ABC was apparently modeled after a very early German standard or the standard used in Austria before fanciers there adopted the revised German standard. Contrary to the German standard in effect in the mid-1930s, the ABC standard specified exact proportions for the Boxer's head and body, and judges were required to measure the dogs when judging. The standard also faulted white markings above the shoulder line and considered "plain" Boxers—those with no white markings at all—to be even better, which reflected the Austrian preference for these types of dogs. The founding members of the ABC who submitted the initial standard were not prominent breeders at the time and had primarily Austrian imports. Most breeders, on the contrary, were using the German standard, which was in use in most countries, and importing German dogs who conformed to that standard.

Something had to be done. In February 1938, Philip Stockmann, Chief German Breed Warden and owner (with his wife Friederun) of the vom Dom Boxer kennel, was brought to the US to judge Boxers at Westminster. He and John Wagner, owner of Mazelaine Kennels, translated the German breed standard, and the translation was used to revise the ABC standard. The AKC approved the revision in May 1938. The revised standard eliminated the use of exact measurements and proportions and allowed "flash" (white) on the face, chest, belly, and legs. Additional revisions have been made to the breed standard since then, and the current version became effective on March 30, 2005.

In 1939, the ABC was incorporated as a not-for-profit corporation in New York with Richard C. Kettles assuming the post of AKC Delegate, which he held for 16 years. The first two

member clubs of the ABC were the Mid-West Boxer Club and Eastern Boxer Club. That same year also saw the first printing of John P. Wagner's *The Boxer*, which was the long-standing bible for Boxer breeders, reprinted several times between 1939 and 1952. Wagner's extensive knowledge came from a decade of breeding and his close contacts with German breeders, especially the Stockmanns. His Mazelaine kennel often had as many as a hundred dogs in its breeding program and still holds the record for producing the most champions—more than 130—owned or bred.

Beginning in September of 1939, World War II put an end to the importation of Boxers from Europe and broke off contact between breeders on both sides of the Atlantic. Fortunately, the Boxer had already established himself firmly among American dogs and their fanciers. Breeding continued, additional Boxer clubs were formed, and more Boxers assumed their places in American homes and hearts.

Four Boxers have won Best in Show at Westminster:
- Champion Warlord of Mazelaine in 1947
- Champion Mazelaine Zazarac Brandy in 1949
- Champion Bang Away of Sirrah Crest in 1951
- Champion Arriba's Prima Donna in 1970

Boxers also hold the following Westminster records:
- Most Group wins—23
- Most consecutive Group wins—5 (1954 through 1958)
- Most Group placements—46
- Most consecutive Group placements—19 (1940 through 1958)

CHARACTERISTICS 2
O F   T H E   B O X E R

A well-bred Boxer is characterized by physical and behavioral traits common to the breed. Serious dog breeders create and maintain a breed by choosing animals who possess the traits needed to perform a specific function or set of functions. If you're looking for a pet, you may wonder why the original purpose of the breed matters to you; after all, you don't plan to ask your Boxer to hunt wild boar or fight other animals! But it is important to understand the traits that make Boxers who they are, because although a Boxer may be the ideal companion canine if you channel his intelligence and energy, he isn't everyone's ideal pet. Let's look at the typical Boxer's traits.

STANDARD TRAITS OF THE BOXER

Form Follows Function

The physical traits of each breed of dog developed as devoted breeders selected those aspects of physical form that helped the dogs perform their functions in partnership with people. It takes many generations of selective breeding to establish a breed, as well as continued attention to careful selection to maintain the traits and talents for which it was developed. Eventually, breeders and other fanciers of a breed write a document called a breed standard that defines the physical, mental, and behavioral characteristics they seek in their dogs. The breed standard also identifies traits that are acceptable but not desirable, and traits that are considered detrimental to the breed and therefore prevent a dog from being bred or disqualify him from competition in conformation shows.

Boxer breed standards have been established by the American Kennel Club (AKC) and other registries. In this chapter, we'll see how the AKC breed standard for the Boxer, written by members of the American Boxer Club (ABC) using the German breed standard as a model, defines the ideal member of the breed. (You will find the complete AKC standard, as well as the complete Kennel Club (UK) standard, in the appendix.)

Physical Traits of the Boxer

The Boxer is a medium-sized, muscular animal. The breed standard specifies that the ideal size for an adult bitch (female) is 21 to 23.5 inches at the withers (the highest point where the shoulder blades meet), and for an adult dog (male), 22.5 to 25 inches. There is no disqualification from the show ring for heights outside the preferred range, although females over the maximum and males under the minimum are not desirable. Bitches range in weight from 50 to 65 pounds, while dogs range from 65 to 80 pounds.

Overall quality and balance are considered more important than strict adherence to the specified height ranges. The Boxer's body is supposed to be "square," meaning that the distance from the point of the prosternum (breastbone) in front of the dog to the back of the thigh should equal the height of the dog from the withers to the ground. The animal should look sturdy and well muscled, and males should have a larger bone structure than females.

One of the traits that attracts many people to the Boxer is his highly expressive face, due in no small part to his intelligent, engaging eyes, which should be dark brown and "not too small, too protruding or too deep-set" in relation to the rest of his head.

Head and Skull

The Boxer is what's known as a "head breed," meaning that in competition in the show ring, the individual's head is an extremely important feature. As the breed standard says, "The beauty of the head depends upon harmonious proportion of muzzle to skull." Ideally, the muzzle is one-third the length from the tip of the nose to the occiput, which is the back-most point of the ridge of bone running along the top of the skull. The width of the muzzle should be two-thirds of the width of the skull. There are folds in the skin from the stop (where the muzzle meets the skull) to the bottom of the muzzle, and when the dog's ears are erect, wrinkles will appear on the forehead, but otherwise the head should be clean (free of wrinkles). Heavy wrinkling or complete lack of wrinkling are both considered faults.

Form is also important in the components that make up the head. The top of the skull should be slightly arched rather than flat, but it should not be rounded. The bony

The form of the Boxer's head is an important part of the AKC breed standard.

ridge of the occiput should not be prominent, and the skull should not be "noticeably broad." The muzzle and skull meet with a definite angle known as the stop, and there is a slight indentation between the eyes, accentuating the expressiveness of the Boxer's face. The cheeks should be flat, not rounded (or cheeky), tapering gently into the muzzle. The Boxer's ears are traditionally cropped into long, tapering points that stand upright from the highest part of the sides of the skull when the dog is alert. In some countries, like the UK, ear cropping has been banned, and Boxers are shown with natural "drop" ears.

The Boxer's upper jaw is broad at the skull and blunt, with barely any tapering toward the front. The Boxer has an undershot bite, meaning that the lower jaw protrudes in front of the upper jaw, curving upward slightly. The lower incisors form a straight row across the front of the jaw, and ideally, the lower canines ("fangs") are set along that same line, giving the lower jaw maximum width. The upper incisors follow a slightly convex line, with the outermost upper incisors lying neatly behind the lower canines. The upper canine teeth align behind the lower canines, enhancing the square, broad look of the muzzle. The Boxer's chin should be visible from both front and side, and the lips should meet evenly in front. The Boxer's nose should be black.

Body

The Boxer's neck should be arched, muscular, and free of dewlaps (dangling skin), and be long enough to balance with his body, blending smoothly into the withers. His topline—the top of his back in silhouette—should be smooth and firm, and should slope slightly downward from front to back. Viewed from the front, his chest should be reasonably wide. From the side, his forechest over the sternum should be visible in front of his shoulders. His brisket (the lower portion of his ribcage) should reach down to his elbows and should measure half the height of the dog. His ribcage should be long and the ribs well arched but not round. The Boxer's shoulders should be long and sloping and muscular without being loaded (overmuscled). The upper arm should form almost a right angle to the shoulder blade. The dog's elbows should be neither too close nor too far from the ribcage to ensure free and efficient movement.

The Boxer's back should be short and muscular, including the loins (the area between the back end of the rib cage and the hips). The croup—the portion of the back from the top of the hips to the base of the tail—should be flat and broad and should slope slightly downward toward the rear. The Boxer's tail is set high and carried up and is traditionally docked. Viewed from the side, the Boxer should have a slight tuck up, with the belly curving gracefully up behind the ribs.

The breed standard also describes in detail how the front and rear legs and feet should be put together to enable the dog to move well and do his job with maximum efficiency and minimal risk of fatigue or injury. When seen from the front, the Boxer's long, straight, muscular forelegs should be parallel. The pastern—the portion of the leg between the paw and the long leg bone or femur—should appear strong and should slant only slightly forward to the foot. The Boxer's feet should point straight ahead and be compact, with nicely arched toes. The dog's hindquarters should be strong and well-muscled, with long, broad, curved thighs. The angle of the stifle (knee), where the long bones of the upper and lower hind leg meet, should equal the angle in front where the long bones of the shoulder blade and arm (foreleg) meet, and should be close to 90 degrees. When seen from behind, the hind legs should appear straight up and down, and from the side, the leg below the hock (the next joint below the stifle, or knee) should be perpendicular to the ground or very slightly sloped toward the rear. The dewclaws (the small toes and nails found on the inside of the front legs above the paws) may be removed. Boxers have no rear dewclaws.

Coat

The Boxer's short coat lies close to the skin and comes in two acceptable colors: fawn and brindle. Fawn ranges in shade from light tan to tawny to a rich mahogany or "stag red." Brindle, which is caused by an overlay of black on the base color, ranges from very light black stripes over fawn to black stripes so heavy and close together that the underlying fawn barely shows through. A black mask darkens the Boxer's face, although white markings, if present, may replace the black on part of the face.

White markings are allowed on the face, legs, chest, and underside as long as they cover no more than one-third of the dog's entire coat, and are "of such distribution as to enhance the dog's appearance." White markings on the body proper, other than the underside, are considered undesirable.

Movement

Sound movement in dogs is assessed primarily at the trot, in which the opposite front and rear legs move together (left front with right hind, right front with left hind) in a two-beat gait. Correct structure and soundness are easier to observe at the trot because the gait is by nature symmetrical and balanced. A working dog must be able to move efficiently, so the Boxer breed standard defines correct movement as consisting of a "smoothly efficient, level-backed, ground covering stride with powerful drive emanating from a freely operating rear." The front legs do not provide power for forward motion but must extend forward with sufficient reach so that they don't interfere with free movement of the hind legs. The Boxer's movement should be smooth, and the elbows should move straight

The term "balanced" is used frequently to describe the overall appearance of the correctly constructed Boxer. Balance refers to the proportions that breeders find desirable for the dog to perform his job, particularly the appearance and relative proportions of the parts of the head, head to body, and height to length. It is also sometimes used to refer to the equality of the angles of the joints between the long bones in the front and hind legs.

Boxers are usually fawn or brindle in color.

alongside the ribs, turning neither in nor out. You should be able to run a straight line from the shoulder through the leg to the foot, and as the dog's speed increases, that line should converge toward an imaginary line on the ground parallel to the center line of the dog in order to maintain balance.

Temperament

Temperament, a dog's fundamental tendency to display friendliness, reserve, aggression, stability, and other traits, is an essential part of the Boxer. Dignity and self-confidence coupled with playfulness or courage when appropriate have made the Boxer a popular and much-loved companion over the years. The breed standard refers to the Boxer as a "hearing guard dog," meaning that he is closely attuned to the sounds in his environment and alert to the presence of potential threats. He's willing to defend his home and hearth if necessary, but he should not be aggressive or vicious. With his own family he is loyal, playful, and affectionate. With strangers, the Boxer may be restrained at first, but he warms up once he knows everything is as it should be. Shyness, and lack of alertness and dignity, are considered faults.

What About White Boxers?

It's not uncommon for fawn or brindle parents with white markings to produce a puppy who is completely white or predominantly white with fawn or brindle patches (called checked or parti-colored). This excessive white occurs when the genes that produce acceptable white markings on the face, chest, belly, and legs "go crazy," extending the white onto the dog's body.

White Boxers have been a part of the breed since its beginning. Although some sources claim that infusions of Bulldog genes into Boxers in the 1890s are responsible, others insist that white Boxers were around even earlier. In fact, as we saw in the last chapter, the first dog registered in the Boxer stud book in 1904 was sired by a white Bulldog.

Regardless of when these dogs first showed up, white was considered an acceptable color in the breed's early days. German breeders used white Boxers in their breeding programs, and the German Boxer Club registered them until 1925, when they were banned as unsuitable for their primary function as guard dogs. Much later, health

Sometimes fawn or brindle parents can produce a predominantly white puppy.

problems associated with excessive white were considered grounds for not breeding white Boxers.

Although these pups have normal dark eyes and noses, showing that they are not albinos (who lack all pigment in the skin, hair, and eyes), they may have certain health issues due to their color. Those who lack pigment in their skin as well as their hair need to be protected from sunburn. Many white or partly white Boxers are completely or partially deaf (see Chapter 8), and in rare cases, the dog's vision may be affected.

As a buyer, you need to be aware that a responsible breeder may offer a white puppy for sale as a pet. However, the manner in which she presents that puppy and handles the terms of the sale will tell you a lot about her ethics as a Boxer breeder. First, white Boxer puppies are not "rare," as sometimes claimed by unscrupulous people; it's estimated that about a quarter of the pups from parents with white markings may be white or partially white. Second, although the American Kennel Club (AKC) will register any puppy whose parents are AKC registered, the American Boxer Club (ABC) policy forbids its members to register white Boxers with the AKC or to use white Boxers for breeding. The ABC does not, however, encourage or condone culling of white puppies by euthanasia—they should instead be spayed or neutered and thus effectively removed from the gene pool.

DO BOXERS MAKE GOOD PETS?

Unfortunately, people sometimes choose a dog by looking only at his virtues, and in the right home, the Boxer has many. But if you're thinking of adding a Boxer to your family, you must remember that he is classified as a member of the Working Group, and for good reason. He is instinctively alert and intelligent as befits his history as a guard dog, hunting companion, and war-time messenger, jobs that require nearly inexhaustible energy, courage, strength, determination, a high tolerance for pain, and the ability to solve problems on his own. When those traits are understood and properly managed with exercise, training, and a sense of humor, they make for an outstanding companion dog. When misunderstood or mismanaged, the same traits create a nightmare for the owner and potential disaster for the dog. All too many Boxers wind up in rescue programs and shelters because of the very traits for which the breed is known. Let's see specifically how some of these traits translate into pet behavior.

Behavioral and Personality Traits

The typical Boxer craves human affection and is happiest when he's with his people. He's an all-around companion dog, happily fulfilling his role as playmate, buddy, and if necessary, protector. Is he the perfect dog? Some of his fans think so, and in the right environment, he is. But the typical Boxer's fundamental physical and mental traits also make for behaviors that aren't suited to all people or environments. In fact, most Boxers who lose their homes and end up in rescue or shelter situations are perfectly normal representatives of their breed. Their "problem behaviors" are problematic only because the dogs were in the wrong environments. Let's look at some behavioral and personality traits that Boxer owners should expect and be willing and able to manage.

Emotional Stability

A well-bred Boxer is very stable emotionally and will take most things in stride. These are loving, social dogs, and they are happiest when they are with their families. Relegating a Boxer to isolation in the backyard is not only shameful, but it will lead to undesirable behaviors in most cases. Boxers are usually very patient with children, but children also need to be taught to respect the dog, and interaction between young children and any dog should be closely supervised. Although he is alert, the Boxer is not nervous or prone to excessive barking, although some individuals may display these behaviors under some circumstances.

Trainability

All dogs need training to be at their best in human company. Training gives your dog the information he needs to do what you want and avoid doing what you don't want, and it

Dignity and self-confidence coupled with playfulness describe the Boxer's temperament.

establishes the trainer—you—as a leader deserving of respect. Training will also give your dog more confidence in himself and in you. Teaching respect does not mean that you should manhandle or hit your dog. On the contrary, there's no reason ever to hurt any dog in the name of training. If you can meet the challenges of training with a sense of humor and respect for the dog's canine heritage using modern motivational training methods, you'll build a relationship of trust and get much farther much faster.

Even with training, though, the Boxer can be a handful, especially when young. Never trust your dog off leash except in a safely confined area. The high drive and enthusiasm for life that he possesses in abundance can lead him into trouble in the wrong environment. Some Boxers will chase anything

Boxers are high-energy dogs who need a lot of physical exercise to keep them happy and healthy.

that moves—squirrels, cats, other dogs, and sometimes joggers, bicycles, or children—and ignore frantic attempts to call them back. This behavior can be simply annoying if it takes you an hour to catch up with your dog, or it can be devastating if he runs into the path of a car, picks a fight with the wrong dog, nips or jumps on someone, or becomes lost. Boxers are also prone to attacks of "the zoomies," giddy running in loops and circles with no destination except a heck of a good time. For his own good and yours, your Boxer must be on leash or safely confined at all times.

Manageability

The Boxer's strength and high tolerance for pain or discomfort can make him a challenge to manage. If you're trying to train him or take him for a walk on his leash, he may not even notice a tug that would stop a more sensitive dog in his tracks. His high intelligence and excellent problem-solving ability make him adept at sports, tricks, and other productive pursuits when he's guided by a competent trainer, but if left undirected, he'll likely use his intellectual and physical abilities to become an escape artist and to redecorate your home and yard.

When dog fanciers talk about "high energy" dogs, they often mean dogs with way more energy than many people can or want to deal with. A 70-pound whirling dervish of a young, happy Boxer is a handful and can be a challenge to even the most dedicated Boxer owner. Pent-up energy coupled with boredom can make for annoying and destructive behaviors like digging, jumping, chewing, and barking if you don't give your Boxer more suitable outlets for his energy and intelligence. The normal high energy of a young Boxer is often wrongly labeled hyperactivity, but in fact it is a normal behavioral trait of the breed. Boxers, especially Boxer puppies and adolescents, are exuberant.

Trying to suppress a Boxer's energy and enthusiasm is usually frustrating for dog and person alike, and ineffective as well. On the other hand, if you can keep your Boxer busy with activities that channel his energy into appropriate alternatives, he can be a terrific companion for you and your family. Lots of active play, like retrieving, going for long walks, and jogging, will certainly help. If you have the time and inclination to train for formal dog sports, Boxers can and do perform well in obedience, agility, flyball, and flying disk sports, where their athletic abilities can be used to negotiate obstacles and pursue flying objects. Tracking puts your dog's fine nose to work and expends energy as you follow scent trails together.

The bottom line is that the Boxer is not the right dog for an owner who cannot direct his energy into acceptable behaviors. So before you rush to join the ranks of Boxer owners, please think carefully about the whole dog, not just the sweet guy sitting at your feet by the fire. It takes both a dog and a person or family to make a lasting canine-human relationship, and the would-be owner's traits are at least as important as those of the dog. You must suit your Boxer just as he must suit you. For everyone's sake, be realistic and choose carefully.

Boxers and Kids

Kids and dogs...what could be a more natural combination? A child with a dog learns about love, friendship, and responsibility, but please don't bring a dog into your home if your child is the only one who wants one. The whole family should be involved in the decision to get a dog. Even if some family members won't be directly involved with the dog as much as others, if any one person—especially a parent—resents the dog's presence, it's a good idea to resolve that issue before adding a four-footed family member.

If you got your dog as a companion for your children, you need to know that happy canine and child relationships don't happen by accident. Young puppies play rough and have sharp teeth and claws. They aren't born knowing how to behave with their new human companions. They're used to playing with their littermates, and puppies play with their mouths and feet, and they like to make each other squeal. Your puppy needs to learn that teeth do not belong on human skin.

Older dogs and older children don't usually need such close supervision, but both need training. For your dog, that means at least basic obedience training and lots of socialization from puppyhood on. Children should be taught to understand that dogs are not toys but living creatures who feel pain. Don't that assume because a dog and child know one another there's no risk of a bite. Most children who are bitten know the dogs who bite them and are on the dogs' home turf. A child will often take more chances with a dog he knows, and dogs are more confident and more protective in their own homes.

Children also don't automatically know how to "play nice" with puppies and dogs. They need to be taught that ears aren't for pulling and eyes aren't for poking. If you have an adult dog or plan to adopt one, the same rules apply. Too many people assume that nice dogs will put up with anything a kid dishes out. That's not fair to the dog, and it's not necessarily true. All too often we hear about a dog who bit a child "without warning." Very few dogs bite without warning, but if the child doesn't understand the dog's signals, and neither do the adults who should be in charge, the dog may eventually nip.

If you can provide a lifetime of love and proper care, is a Boxer the right dog for your children? Lots of Boxers do live successfully with kids, but you need to consider carefully the traits that can make them less than ideal pets for some families. Even though Boxers are not prone to snapping, don't expect a dog to put up with endless poking, prodding, ear pulling, or teasing. That's unrealistic and unfair to both dog and child. Unlike puppies, children are not equipped with instincts that tell them how to recognize canine warnings and submit or back off, and a clash between the two species can be tragic for both.

Children are much more likely than adults to be bitten, and boys are bitten more often than girls. Although ideally dogs shouldn't bite, bites are nearly always provoked by the victim. Your children should be taught how to interact safely

Make sure children understand how to safely play with your Boxer.

and respectfully with your dog. No one should roughhouse or play tug-of-war or other games that encourage your Boxer to grab for things or compete with people of any age for control of "resources" like food, toys, beds, and other furniture. The no roughhousing rule applies especially to children. Although your Boxer should be taught not to guard things from people, your children—especially young ones—also need to learn not to take things away from the dog. They also need to learn not to pull your dog's ears or poke his eyes. All too many people seem to think that a "good" dog will take anything a kid dishes out. That's certainly unfair to the dog, and it's a dangerous assumption.

All interaction between children and puppies should be closely supervised by a responsible adult who is in a position to intervene immediately. You can also greatly reduce the chance that your Boxer will bite by having the dog altered (spayed or neutered). Altering greatly reduces aggression and lowers the risk of a bite in dogs of both sexes.

Keeping Your Child and Dog Safe

Make your child or someone else's child safer by teaching these basic rules for interacting with dogs:

- Don't run up to a dog; walk slowly, and don't scream or yell.
- Always ask the owner before you try to pet a dog you don't know. Some dogs are afraid of strangers or don't like to be petted. If the owner says no, don't try to touch the dog. If the owner says yes, then approach the dog calmly and quietly.
- Always let the dog sniff your open hand before you try to pet him. Never reach over a dog's head or touch him from behind until after he has a chance to sniff you; you may startle him, and he may snap in self-defense. The best place to pet a dog is under his chin or on his chest.
- If a dog tries to get away from you, don't chase him. A frightened dog might bite.
- If you see a dog without a person, don't approach the dog.
- Don't tease a dog. Teasing is mean and may frighten the dog or make him angry. Never yell at a dog, and never pretend to bark or growl at him.
- Don't try to take food, toys, bones, or anything else away from a dog. If your dog has something he shouldn't have, ask an adult to help.
- Don't bother a dog who is eating, sleeping, eliminating, or taking care of puppies.
- Don't stare at a dog's eyes, especially if the dog doesn't know you.
- Don't run away from a dog. If you're running and a dog chases you, stop, stand still, and be quiet. If the dog comes close to you, "be a tree"—cross your arms with your hands on your shoulders. Don't look at the dog.
- If a dog barks, growls, or shows you his teeth, he's telling you that he might bite you if you come closer. If you see a dog acting like that, look away from the dog's face and walk very slowly sideways until the dog relaxes or you're out of sight.
- If a dog attacks you, "be a ball"—get down on your knees, and curl up with your face tucked onto your legs and your arms around your head. Lie still—don't move or scream.
- If a dog bites you, tell an adult right away. If you don't know the dog, try to remember where you were when he bit you, what the dog looked like, where the dog lives if you know, which way he went after he bit you, and who else saw him bite you.
- If you see dogs fighting, don't try to stop them! Stay away from the dogs, and find an adult to help.
- If you see an injured dog, don't touch him. Find an adult to help.

Environment

The best environment for a Boxer isn't so much a location as it is a lifestyle. As we've seen, he needs an owner who will see to it that he gets the physical and mental stimulation he needs to channel his boundless enthusiasm. Can a Boxer live happily in an apartment? Possibly, if his person takes him for long, long walks, trains him in basic obedience and in some other activity to challenge his mind, and finds safe outlets for him to use up his energy. Can he live happily with a walk around the block and long hours confined indoors? Probably not. And if your Boxer isn't happy, chances are you won't be happy, either. All that energy has to go somewhere. If you don't direct it, your dog will!

Whether you live in the city or the country, it's up to you to keep your Boxer safe.

On the other hand, a Boxer who lives in the country without training, control, and lots of interaction with his people will be likely to wander or get into serious trouble during his undirected adventures. He needs a safe place to play, as well as supervision, to keep him safe. The modern world holds many hazards for a dog on his own, and it's your job to keep him safe, no matter where you live.

It's also your job to honor your Boxer's essential role as a companion animal. Boxers love to be with their people, and your dog belongs with you in your home, where he can see you, hear you, and smell you with every breath he takes. Give him these things—training, exercise, companionship, and love—and you will be rewarded many times over every time you look into his big brown eyes.

3 PREPARING
F O R   Y O U R   B O X E R

Y ou've decided to get a Boxer! That's a huge decision, but you have more choices to make in order to find the right dog and make sure you have everything you need to get off to a great start with your new buddy.

PRELIMINARY DECISIONS

Puppy or Adult?

There's nothing cuter or sweeter or funnier than a baby dog, which is probably why most people don't think about the downside of raising a puppy or the advantages of bringing home a more mature Boxer.

A puppy will need plenty of exercise every single day, as well as lots of supervision to keep him out of trouble. He'll probably urinate on your carpet and rip up a few things. In a few short weeks he'll become an adolescent, and although he won't whine to use the family car, he will question authority. During this period, which can last two years or longer, your young Boxer will need training and activities to challenge his mind as well as his body. If you don't guide and control him, he definitely won't be the dog of your dreams.

Both nature and nurture affect how your puppy will mature. Raising a puppy lets you influence his development to some extent because you control his socialization, training, nutrition, exercise, and other experiences. However, your puppy's genetic makeup, something you have no influence over, also affects the dog he will become. If you're dedicated to proper puppy training and rearing, realize that it won't all be fun, have a responsible breeder to guide you through the rough spots, and have a sense of humor, then a puppy may be a good choice. But if the pain will outweigh the pleasure, you might be happier with an adult.

When you choose an adult Boxer, what you see is pretty much what you get. If he's been neglected, you can expect him to improve with better food, care, and training, but the essential dog is already apparent. But many people wonder, will an adult dog bond to me? Absolutely! Human beings cherish the idea of the utterly faithful dog, true unto death, but most dogs are quite happy to love the one they're with if they get the care and attention they need. Being replaceable is humbling, but it's good to know that if something were to happen to you, your dog could still live a happy doggy life.

Deciding whether to purchase a puppy or adult Boxer is an important decision.

Male or Female?

Many people think that females are gentle, sweet, and motherly, and therefore make better pets than males, who are supposedly independent and prone to wander. In reality, intact (unspayed) bitches can experience serious mood swings due to cyclical hormonal changes, and they can be aggressive and very protective of their young. On the other hand, male dogs can be steady, loyal companions.

Other than genes and upbringing, your dog's reproductive status exerts the strongest influence on his or her personality and behavior. The hormones that propel sexual behavior are powerful, and sexually intact Boxers of both genders are much more prone to wander, bite, mark indoors and out, and indulge in other annoying behaviors than are their neutered brethren. If you want a stable, affectionate, devoted pet, look for a male or female Boxer with a sound temperament, socialize and train him or her properly, and have him or her neutered.

The Best Time to Bring a Puppy Home

Some people say that a puppy must come to his new home at exactly seven weeks of age or he'll never bond to his new family. Nonsense! The "seven-week myth" is based on a misunderstanding of research that showed that puppies who don't have positive contact with people—any people—by the seventh week will have trouble bonding to people throughout their lives. In fact, during the short time from the seventh to twelfth weeks of a puppy's life, it is critical that the pup meet lots of friendly people and animals if he's to develop proper social skills. However, the people he meets do not have to be the ones with whom he'll spend his life.

Puppies go through several developmental fear imprint periods, the first occurring at about eight weeks. Anything that frightens or hurts the puppy during these periods may remain frightening to him throughout his life, so it's important to shelter him from bad experiences at this time. Because the first fear period is often the most influential, some breeders keep their pups until they have passed this critical time.

If you're buying a puppy, ask the source how the litter has been handled. Each puppy should have spent one-on-one time every day with at least one person and begun housetraining no later than the seventh week. Puppies can begin to learn to sit, lie down, stand, come on command, and walk nicely on leash. It will take a few weeks for them to master these lessons, but the sooner you begin, the faster they will learn not only the individual command, but *how* to learn as well. If you want a well-adjusted adult Boxer, *do not* get one who hasn't been handled between the seventh and twelfth weeks, and don't take one home at this age if you can't spend lots of time with him.

BREEDERS

Boxer puppies are darned near irresistible, but it's to your advantage to resist poorly bred puppies. Take your time to find a responsible breeder who is committed to the health and well-being of her own dogs and the Boxer as a breed. You won't be sorry! Such a breeder works hard to breed physically and mentally healthy animals, to make each generation better than the one before, and to give her puppies a good start. She matches dams and sires carefully, provides good prenatal and postnatal care, and closely monitors her puppies and bitches before, during, and after the birth. She socializes her puppies and will try to pick the right puppy for you.

Breeders sometimes have nice older puppies or adults available for adoption. These may be pups who haven't lived up to their early promise for competition or breeding. They may be retired show or breeding dogs who would be happier with one-on-one attention, or they may even be grown-up puppies who have been returned to the breeder due to divorce, illness, or other reasons. If you don't want to tackle puppy raising but the dog's history is important to you, an adult from a breeder may be a good choice.

Finding a Responsible Breeder

Start with the American Boxer Club (ABC) and your local dog clubs—they often maintain directories of breeders. (You can find a list of clubs on the AKC's website.) If you see a Boxer you like, talk to the owner and find out where the dog is from. Attend a dog show or a trial, and

Good breeders are committed to the health and well-being of their Boxers.

purchase a catalog—it lists the names of the dogs and their breeders, as well as the names and addresses of their owners. If you see a Boxer you like, talk to the owner or mark your catalog and contact the breeder later. You can locate many breeders simply by searching the Internet for their names and the names of their kennels or individual dogs.

Why look for breeders whose dogs are competing if you just want a nice pet? For one excellent reason: Most responsible breeders participate in activities that test their dogs' instincts, abilities, and quality. A good breeder strives in every litter to produce her next hotshot dog, but even in a litter from high-achieving parents, some of the pups just won't have what it takes to be competitive. Those puppies are destined to be pets—a fine destiny for a dog! The factors that keep them out of competition are often minor, and you may not see their faults even if the breeder shows you.

You may be able to find a good breeder and well-bred puppy through a newspaper or magazine advertisement, but be careful. Some very appealing ads are placed by some very unappealing people. You'll be investing time, money, and emotions in the dog you bring into your life, and the more carefully you choose your pup's breeder, the happier you'll all be in the end. Keep in mind that a responsible breeder:

- keeps her puppies until they're at least seven weeks old;
- answers questions happily;
- asks you lots of questions;
- welcomes you to visit and meet her dogs;
- belongs to one or more dog clubs;
- screens all her breeding dogs for hereditary diseases;
- acknowledges that inherited problems occur and does not claim that her dogs' bloodlines are free of health problems (there's no such thing as a "clean line");
- won't sell you a breedable dog until you prove that you're responsible;
- tells you about the challenges of owning a Boxer;
- handles and socializes her puppies;
- keeps her dogs in a clean environment;
- knows every dog by name, and every puppy as an individual;
- happily refers you to her previous buyers;
- asks for and checks your references;
- does not sell "purebred but unregistered" puppies and does not charge extra for "papers";

Visiting Breeders

When you're ready to visit breeders, don't plan back-to-back visits—it's extremely easy to carry diseases and parasites from one location to another, even if everything looks clean. Between visits be sure to shower and change into clean clothes, including your shoes.

A breeder's puppies should look clean and healthy.

• does not pressure you to buy a puppy—in fact, she makes you prove you're good enough to own one!

For a responsible breeder, dog breeding is not a business in the usual sense, and the number you call rings into her home. She probably has several dogs and a human family, a job, and other interests and obligations. Call at a reasonable hour, and offer to call back if it's not a good time for her. Don't expect a breeder who doesn't know you to return long-distance calls at her expense. Many breeders have websites that you can locate with a search engine that will answer a lot of your questions. Quite a few also prefer initial contacts by e-mail so they can answer when it's convenient for them.

Ask questions and be prepared to answer some. Breeders sometimes speak "doglish," so ask for clarification if you don't understand something. Trust your instincts. You should be entering a long-term relationship with this person, so if you're uncomfortable, thank her for her time and move to the next breeder on your list.

Beware of anyone who breeds more than two or three different breeds or who has bounced frequently and repeatedly from one breed to another. A novice breeder who is well informed is much better than someone with years of irresponsible breeding behind her, but experience does have

value. If the person is new to breeding Boxers, you'll have decide whether her answers to your questions give you confidence in her knowledge of the breed. Ask why she bred this bitch to this dog, and find out what strengths and weaknesses the individuals and their bloodlines possess. Even if you don't know a lot about Boxer pedigrees, you'll be able to tell whether the breeder seems to know about the puppies' ancestors. Serious breeders can recite pedigrees from memory, and they know what desirable and undesirable traits various ancestors are likely to pass along.

Find out what the breeder's long-term goals are and how the litter you're considering moves her toward that goal. Does she want to produce winning show dogs, agility stars, or all-around, versatile Boxers? If this is the case, stick around. If she breeds to make some money or because her Boxer is so darn cute, though, run the other way.

A responsible breeder will show you registration papers, health clearances, title certificates, pedigrees, and other paperwork related to the litter. If she doesn't offer, ask to see documents supporting any claims she makes about the dogs. Don't buy from any breeder who can't show the paperwork or who resents your request or says you can see the paperwork after you buy the puppy. That would be like a seller offering to tell you the age and make of a car after you pay for it.

Choosing the Puppy

Before you buy a Boxer puppy, meet the breeder's dogs to get an idea of their general personalities. Ask for references of people who have purchased dogs from the breeder, and follow up. Find out whether their dogs have exhibited any temperament problems. Good temperament is no accident. Like correct head structure and physical health, temperament is in large measure inherited. In fact, a breeder should select breeding dogs based on proper temperament as well as other traits.

When deciding on a puppy, you should be able to meet the puppy's dam (mother). Motherhood is hard work so she may not look her best, but a well-cared-for dam will not look exhausted, malnourished, or ill. She may be concerned for her puppies, but she should accept your presence when the breeder vouches for you, and she should be reasonably friendly when away from the puppies. If the sire (father) is present, you should meet him, too. If he lives elsewhere, the breeder should be able to show you pictures and copies of his health clearances, titles certificates, pedigree, and registration. Meet other relatives of the litter if possible. If you don't like the puppy's parents, grandparents, and other relatives, don't buy the puppy.

The facilities should be clean and in good repair. The dogs should look healthy and well cared for and have room to move around and play. They should also have access to fresh water. Mutual love and respect should be obvious between the breeder and her dogs, and she should be able to share a lot of information about each puppy in the litter.

You're going to get all kinds of advice about how to choose *your* puppy. Let the puppy choose you, says your brother-in-law—and you might wind up with a dominant pup who doesn't suit you. Someone else may recommend puppy temperament and aptitude tests, but tests haven't been proven to predict adult behavior accurately. A good breeder watches and interacts with her puppies for weeks; you only see them for a few hours. This is why it's important to tell your breeder what you want and don't want in your dog, and let her choose your puppy, or two or three from which you can choose.

Signs of a Healthy 7- to 12-Week-Old Puppy

A healthy puppy:
- is solid and well proportioned;
- is neither too thin nor potbellied (he may be malnourished or infested with roundworms);
- has soft, glossy fur;
- has no red, itchy, or bald spots, and no fleas;
- has a clean anal area;
- has bright, clear eyes;
- has pink gums and healthy breath smelling only of the slightly musky odor of "puppy breath;"
- has a correct bite and properly aligned jaws;
- has a clean, damp nose with no sign of discharge;
- breathes without sneezing, coughing, or wheezing;
- has clean ears;
- moves well, with no signs of lameness or other problems;
- is happy and playful—except when he's asleep.

If you are making the final choice, watch the puppies play with their dam and littermates alone and with people. Don't pick the pushiest puppy, and don't choose the pushover. If a puppy shows no interest in people, he may be more independent than you want. He should be confident but not a bully. He should show interest in objects tossed across the floor. Single encounters can fool you, though—if the

Adopting an adult Boxer into your family can be a wonderful option.

puppies have played all afternoon, the one you think is calm and quiet may actually be a hooligan who just happens to be worn out. That's why it's important to trust your breeder.

Contracts and Guarantees

There is no such thing as a standard puppy sale contract. Assume nothing—read the contract carefully and be sure you understand the terms. Consider having a disinterested, experienced breeder, exhibitor, or attorney look at the contract before you sign.

Your puppy should be guaranteed healthy when you take him home. Most breeders cover the first 48 to 72 hours, during which time you should have your own vet examine the pup. Some breeders also offer guarantees against inherited diseases, but it's important to understand that a guarantee *does not* mean that your puppy cannot develop a problem. It does mean that the breeder is confident about her breeding choices and will do something to compensate you if a problem appears. Your best bet is to buy from a breeder who does everything humanly possible to breed healthy puppies, but to also realize that with living things there's always some risk.

Few breeders offer financial compensation if something goes wrong with the puppy you chose, but many offer a "replacement" puppy. However, dogs aren't interchangeable like televisions, so be clear about the terms. Will you have to return the first puppy? Is there a time limit? Will the second puppy be closely related to the first? If you don't like the terms or if the terms are unclear and the breeder won't clarify them in writing, look for another breeder.

ADOPTION OPTIONS

If you don't want to pay the price for a well-bred Boxer, why not adopt from a rescue group or shelter? You and the dog you adopt will both win, and you won't support irresponsible breeding. Fine adult Boxers can always be found looking for homes. Let's see where they are.

Purebred Rescue Programs

Rescue involves people and groups that take in and foster homeless dogs and then place them in new homes. Rescuers are volunteers who donate time, knowledge, dog-handling skills, and living quarters as a labor of love.

Here are some questions to ask if you are thinking of adopting an adult Boxer:
- Why is he available?
- What do you know about this dog's history?
- Does he have any behavior problems?
- Has he ever bitten anyone?
- Is he friendly with other dogs? (Cats?)
- Is he housetrained?
- Has he had any obedience training?
- What health tests and vaccinations has he had?
- Does he have any problems getting around?

Why do Boxers need to be rescued? Some have lost their owners to misfortune. Others were found as strays or removed from puppy mills or other abusive situations. But most Boxers in rescue are there just for being who they are meant to be: smart, bold, energetic dogs with tremendous *joie de vivre*. Their first owners chose the breed for the wrong reasons and couldn't manage the real-life dog. The typical rescue is an adolescent or young adult, although puppies or seniors are available occasionally. Most of the dogs have no real behavioral problems, and they thrive when given the training, exercise, and care they need.

Good rescue programs evaluate each dog's temperament, behavior, and training needs while he is fostered in a household environment, and they will not place dogs with known histories of biting, aggression, or severe behavioral problems. However, you should still be sure to ask about the procedures and policies of any group you contact. Volunteers usually begin basic training and encourage or require adopters to take their dogs to obedience classes. Rescued dogs are generally given physical examinations, and potential adopters are advised about possible health problems. Reputable rescuers always require that rescued dogs be neutered.

To adopt, you'll fill out an application, provide references, and agree to a home visit. You'll sign an adoption contract agreeing to provide proper care and to return the dog to the organization if you can't keep him. You'll pay an adoption fee or be asked for a donation. Please be generous. Without private support, organized rescue programs would cease to exist.

Update your dog's rescuers occasionally. The rescue volunteer's best reward is knowing that a dog who passed through her hands is doing well and making someone happy.

Shelters and Pounds

Boxers show up in shelters for the same reasons they find their way to rescues. Adopting a dog from a shelter can certainly be rewarding, but don't adopt the first cute face you see. If you're looking for a Boxer but don't know the breed well, take someone with you who does. Shelter staff usually consist of dedicated animal lovers, but not all of them are able to identify breeds accurately, and lots of dogs are misidentified in shelters.

When you find a dog who interests you, ask lots of questions about his known history, how he's been evaluated, who did the evaluation, and what was included. If you are uneasy about the dog's behavior, walk away. If you lack confidence in the shelter personnel's ability to assess the dog and to give you knowledgeable advice, find another shelter or a rescue group.

Health can also be an issue, depending on the resources available. Some well-funded shelters have all incoming animals examined by a veterinarian, but many can't afford to offer more than basic evaluation and care.

A well-run shelter will be reasonably clean. Dogs awaiting adoption may be thin and in need of a bath, but they should look fairly healthy. Be cautious about adopting a dog who appears to be ill, no matter how sorry you feel for him—you don't want to bring home an infectious disease. If you want a specific dog but have concerns about his condition, take him to your vet for a thorough exam and possible quarantine *before* you take him home. Many problems can be fixed with proper food, exercise, and care, but it would be tragic if your good intentions harmed another dog in your home or neighborhood.

Many dogs in shelters are lonely, depressed, or frightened. A little time in a quiet place and a few treats may help break the ice. The prospective adoptee should meet your whole family before you decide, but don't overwhelm a nervous dog with a raucous first meeting. Most kids are sympathetic, gentle, and quiet when they understand. Of course, most Boxers are very outgoing and confident, so caution on the dog's part may not be an issue at all!

Private Adoptions

People place dogs in new homes for all sorts of reasons, some of them perfectly legitimate. Be cautious, though, about dogs advertised in newspapers or on bulletin boards; some people have no qualms about "forgetting" to mention health or behavioral issues. If lack of proper care or training is to blame, the dog may be fine in the right home. Some problems, though, are serious, so ask questions and pay close attention to the answers.

Ask whether the dog has ever bitten, snapped, or threatened to bite a person and whether he gets along with other animals. Ask to see his veterinary records, and see if he's been on heartworm prevention. If records are unavailable, call the vet who has seen the dog, explain that you are thinking of adopting, and ask if there's anything you need to know. If the dog has no history of health care, ask if you can have the dog examined by your own vet at your expense before you commit to adopting him. Invite the owner along for the ride—she probably won't let you take the dog otherwise. If there's no health care record and you can't have the dog checked out, be alert and use your best judgment.

PET STORES

Some people think first of pet stores when looking for a puppy. A pet store may be convenient, and it may have a puppy whenever you're ready for one, but as with any major purchase, you need to know what you're buying. Reading this book is a start; the more you know about Boxers, the better your chances of getting a healthy puppy with a good disposition. Some people also think that pet store puppies cost less than pups from breeders, but that isn't always the case, and prices also vary from one store to another.

Pet store puppies are often "registered," but if you're interested in an AKC-registered puppy, ask to see the paperwork before you buy. Many people who produce pups for pet stores do not register them with the American Kennel Club. Be aware, too, that registration papers indicate nothing about quality. They only show that the parents and litter were registered with the organization that issued the papers.

Naturally, you want a healthy puppy no matter where you buy, and not all pet stores obtain their puppies from good sources. Ask the same questions you would ask a breeder to increase the chances that the puppy you buy is healthy and will remain that way throughout his life. You should see the same types of documentation, including a pedigree, the name and address of the breeder, and proof of screening tests for inherited diseases.

PREPARING YOUR HOME AND YARD

Your new Boxer is coming home! You're probably very excited, but there is a lot of work to be done to prepare.

No matter where you get your Boxer, make sure you do your homework and get a dog who is right for you and your family.

Your home can be dangerous as well as tempting for a puppy, so begin by putting breakables out of reach. Also, items like dangling tablecloths or runners are tailormade for a tug, and shoes, plants, and decorations look like toys to the uneducated canine eye.

Many plants are toxic, so keep your Boxer out of gardens and compost heaps, and put houseplants out of reach. If you use chemicals on your lawn, follow directions for drying time before letting your Boxer outside. If you use a lawn service, check with a poison control site about safety—don't rely on the people who apply the chemicals for accurate information. Store poisons meant for pests, as well as antifreeze, securely. Clean up spills thoroughly. Dispose of containers for hazardous products where your dog can't get to them.

Dogs of all ages can die from swallowing all sorts of unlikely things, like pins, needles, yarn, razor blades, cigarette butts, and nylon stockings. Chocolate, grapes, raisins, medicines, vitamins, and tobacco products can also kill. Teach your kids to put things away; they're usually more willing when the puppy's well-being is at stake (not to mention the well-being of any toys he may chew). Keep electrical and telephone wires out of reach, or run them through specially designed sheaths or PVC pipe cut to size.

Before welcoming your new Boxer into your home, make your house and yard dog-safe.

SUPPLIES

Although you can get by without a lot of extras, raising a puppy or settling in an adult dog will be a lot easier on both of you if you have the right equipment on hand before your new buddy arrives. Let's look at a basic shopping list.

Crate

A crate (sometimes called a carrier or cage) is the best tool for keeping your puppy and belongings safe. It is also useful when housetraining, traveling, and confining your dog if he is injured or ill. A crate will give your dog a safe haven when you're not home, and it will help prevent

Shopping List

The following are some basic supplies your new Boxer will need:
- crate
- bedding
- collar
- leash
- safe toys
- food
- bowls
- treats
- brush
- nail clipper

unwanted behaviors by keeping your dog confined when you can't watch him. Not only will that safeguard your belongings, but it will keep you pup from hurting himself on things he shouldn't touch. He will also be much safer traveling in a crate than he would be loose in a vehicle. Some people resist the idea of crating, but most dogs enjoy the den-like environment of their crates.

Dog crates come in wire, plastic, and aluminum, on wheels, with handles, and in various colors and sizes. Fabric crates are also available but are used primarily for events away from home; they are not recommended for use without reasonable supervision unless you know your dog is quiet in his crate. A Boxer needs a crate approximately 24 inches wide by 36 inches long by 28 inches tall. Be sure the door fits well and latches securely so that paws and teeth can't open it. Most people like to provide bedding in the crate, but if your pup likes to rip things to shreds, forego the bedding until he outgrows his urge to shred.

Collar

Your dog needs at least one collar. An adjustable, quick-release flat nylon collar is a good choice for a Boxer puppy. Nylon collars are inexpensive, come in a kaleidoscope of colors, and are easy to readjust.

The following are some safe collar practices that you should follow when your Boxer is wearing his collar:
- Don't let dogs play or be alone together with collars on—one dog's collar can trap the other dog's jaw or leg, causing serious injuries to one or both.
- You should be able to insert two fingers between the collar and your dog's neck. Check the fit often and readjust or replace the collar when necessary.
- Never use a slip (choke) collar on a puppy—you can severely injure his throat and spine.

Leash

You will need at least one leash. Don't underestimate how quickly your Boxer can get away and be seriously hurt or killed—always leash him when he's not inside walls or a fence. A 4- to 6-foot leather leash $3/4$ of an inch to 1 inch wide is strong, kind to your skin, and effective for training. Many people use nylon leashes, but they are hard on hands

A nylon collar is a good choice for your Boxer puppy.

and can burn or cut if a rambunctious dog winds them around your legs. Chain leashes can injure your puppy or you, and they are ineffective for training.

Identification

Attach an identification tag with your phone number, as well as your dog's rabies and license tags, to his collar, and consider a permanent form of ID as well. Your veterinarian can insert a microchip—a transmitter about the size of a grain of rice—under the skin between your dog's shoulders, or you can have your dog tattooed with an identifying number, normally on the belly or flanks. For more information, check with your veterinarian.

Grooming Supplies

You'll need to get some grooming supplies, including a rubber curry comb for cleaning the coat and removing loose hairs; soft bristle brush for finishing and polishing the coat; nail clippers and possibly a nail grinder or file; a mild shampoo formulated for dogs; and doggy tooth care products. You may also want a flea comb and a tick remover if those pests are a problem where you live.

Toys and Chewies

Some of the most fun items to shop for are toys and chewies. Dogs have individual preferences, and some Boxers are more aggressive chewers than others, so if your Boxer doesn't like one chew toy, try another kind. Well-made chew toys, like Nylabone products, are safer and longer lasting than less expensive ones. Replace chew toys when they develop cracks or sharp points or edges or when they become too small to be safe. Dogs like furry toys and squeaky toys, but beware of plastic eyes, synthetic stuffing, and squeakers that can injure your dog if he swallows them.

Food and Bowls

Even if you receive a starter supply with your dog, you'll need to buy food within a few days. Talk to your breeder, rescuer, or vet about appropriate food for your Boxer. (See Chapter 4 for more information.)

Treats in reasonable amounts are good for training, but too many treats can quickly make your dog chubby, so dole them out sparingly, and watch your dog's weight. Many dogs like carrots and small bits of fruits and other vegetables (but no onion, grapes, and raisins—they're toxic for dogs).

You will also need bowls for food and water. Some dogs develop allergies to plastic bowls, and they can harbor dangerous bacteria. Some ceramic bowls made outside the United States contain lead and other toxins that can leach into food and water. Stainless steel bowls are the best choice because they are sturdy, easy to clean, and resistant to chewing.

SETTLING IN WITH YOUR NEW BOXER

Now let's see what you can do to make settling in easier for both you and your new Boxer.

Puppy's First Few Nights

Your puppy will probably cry for attention and reassurance during his first few nights in your home. If you bring your puppy's crate into your bedroom at night, he'll feel more secure knowing you're nearby, and you'll be able to hear him stirring and take him out to potty during the night, which will speed up the housetraining process.

Take your pup out to potty shortly before bedtime. If he whines or barks in his crate, and you're sure he doesn't need to potty, grit your teeth and ignore him. If he learns that complaining gets him nowhere, he'll quiet down. If he's been asleep and then cries, he probably needs to go out. Carry him out—he may not be able to hold it if he's walking. When he's finished, praise him and put him back in his crate. You'll lose some sleep during the first week or two, but your puppy is just a baby—it's his job to keep his "parents" up for a few nights!

If your puppy can't sleep in your bedroom, place a ticking clock or a radio on low volume near his crate so he doesn't feel completely alone. Expect him to cry the first few nights and to have a few accidents if you can't hear him asking to go out. A puppy's capacity to wait between potty breaks varies by individual, but most puppies can go one hour for each month of age, plus one. So if your pup is four months old, he can probably go about five hours without urinating. Eight hours is about maximum for most adults.

Living Nicely With Others

Dogs organize themselves into a dominance hierarchy in which an alpha dog or bitch is in charge and every group member occupies a specific rank, making him subordinate to pack members who rank higher and are dominant over those who rank lower. Dominance is established by force of personality, not age or sex or size—or species! This hierarchical social system reduces conflict within the group because every dog knows his place.

Many dogs are also territorial. Your dog will mark his territory—your home and yard—by urinating around the perimeter, and if you housetrain him properly, he'll mark only outdoors. He will also defend his territory from intruders, which is why he barks at the mail carrier. If you already have a dog, he may defend his territory against your new puppy or dog, whom he sees as an intruder, but you can reduce the friction with some planning.

Introduce the dogs somewhere you don't usually take your dog so that territory won't be an issue. You need one person to handle each dog, and both dogs should be on leash for control. Let the dogs sniff each other while you talk to them in a quiet but happy voice. Watch their body language. If one dog lowers his front end in a bow and wags his tail, he's inviting the other to play. If one licks the other's mouth and chin, crouches, or rolls over on his back, he's displaying submission, acknowledging the other dog's higher rank. These are good signs.

Hair standing on end, growling, bared teeth, staring, stiff-legged walking, or attempts by one dog to mount the other all signal hostility. If you see these signals, distract the dogs, move them apart, and have them sit or lie down to reinforce your position as alpha. Wait awhile, then try again. Keep encounters short and be alert. If the behavior escalates, separate the dogs again. Some dogs don't like each other in the beginning but eventually become buddies, so don't give up too soon. However, you need to be cautious. Dog fights can be violent, and one or both dogs could be injured if things get out of hand. When the dogs stop checking each other out—or better yet, when they start playing—take them home. Be cautious for at least the first few weeks, though. When you can't supervise the dogs, separate or crate them. Once the dogs are used to one another, use your best judgment about whether they should be trusted together when you're not there to supervise.

If you're getting a puppy, don't leave him alone with an adult dog unless you're absolutely sure about the adult, and even then, give the adult time away from the puppy and private time with you. Puppies are pests, and even a well-socialized adult can get fed up. Puppies younger than four months haven't mastered canine body language or manners, and they may not understand when older dogs tell them to back off. Give each dog his own food bowl and toys, and don't let the pup annoy the older dog when he's eating.

Your Boxer can get along with other animals as long as he's properly socialized and introductions are supervised.

If you have a cat, introduce a new adult Boxer to her very cautiously, and do not allow the dog to chase the cat. Let the cat initiate and control all interactions. If you have a puppy, teach him from the beginning that he may not chase or attack the cat. Set up dog-free areas where your cat can sleep, eat, play, and use the litter box without canine "assistance." Be sure the cat always has an escape route.

TRAVELING WITH YOUR BOXER

Most Boxers like to go where their people go, and there will probably be many times you want to take your dog along, whether you're running up to the corner for a gallon of milk or across the continent to visit Grandma. If you keep a few precautions in mind, there's no reason your Boxer can't do a little traveling by your side.

Traveling by Car

A happy dog with his head out the window and the wind in his face may appeal to us, but letting your Boxer travel loose in a car is risky. Dust and other air-borne debris hitting at the speed of a moving vehicle can cause permanent damage to eyes and ears. A leap from a window or truck bed can kill or injure your dog on impact or get him run over by another vehicle. An unrestrained dog can be thrown if you hit the brakes, hurting himself or someone else.

When traveling with your Boxer by car, he will be much safer in a crate. If you're in an accident, the crate will protect him from injuries and keep him secure in the aftermath. More than one dog has survived a car accident and then been killed or lost when released through an open door. If you're injured, someone will be able to see to your Boxer's care more easily if he's crated.

A doggy seatbelt, if fitted and fastened properly, will also keep your dog from being thrown around in an accident, although it won't protect him as well as a crate. Dogs, like small children, can be injured or killed by a deploying air bag, so don't strap your Boxer into the front seat, no matter how much you enjoy having him beside you.

We all know that a parked car becomes uncomfortable very quickly, even with the windows slightly opened. You may not realize, though, that the temperature can become lethal for your dog in just a few minutes, and brachycephalic (short-faced) breeds like the Boxer are particularly vulnerable to heatstroke. On a hot day, if your dog can't get out of the car with you, leave him safe at home.

Traveling by Air

Thousands of dogs fly every year. Because of his size, your Boxer will travel as cargo unless he's very young and small, in which case he may be able to ride in the cabin in an airline-approved carrier that will fit under a seat.

Your dog will need a health certificate issued by a veterinarian within ten days prior to the flight. He should wear identification, and you should be sure to carry a leash with you. Be aware, too, that airline regulations prohibit flying brachycephalic dogs in hot weather. Check with the airline you plan to use for booking requirements, prices, restrictions, and so on.

If You Can't Take Your Boxer

There are times when our dogs simply can't come along, and fortunately, there are some good alternatives.

Boarding Kennels

A good boarding kennel is a safe alternative to taking your dog along if you choose carefully. Ask for recommendations, and tour the facility ahead of time. Unless you have asked to house more than one dog together, your pup should have a kennel run to himself. The

Practicing Good Traveling Manners

Unfortunately, some people have behaved in ways that have made dogs *canis non grata* in many public places. Most offensive are those who don't clean up after their dogs. Picking up dog poop isn't the most pleasant thing we do for our dogs, but it's not difficult. A quick grab with a plastic bag or glove, a toss in the trash, and you're set.

Be courteous if you are staying in a hotel room with your Boxer. Don't leave your dog alone to bark or cause problems, and bring a sheet to spread over beds or chairs where your dog may rest.

As long as you take some precautions, your Boxer can travel safely with you.

facilities should be clean, and fresh water should always be available. The entire kennel area should be fenced so that if your dog slips out of his run, he'll still be confined. Plans should be in place to handle emergencies and potential disasters and to prevent theft or vandalism. Someone responsible should also be on-site at all times.

Some kennels charge for extra services, so be sure you understand what the basic service includes and how much the extras will cost.

Pet Sitters

You may prefer to hire a pet sitter to care for your dog at home. Some sitters come a specified number of times each day; others stay in your home. Invite the prospective sitter to visit ahead of time to be sure she's comfortable with your pets and vice versa. Ask how often she'll visit and what she's willing to do—feed your Boxer, give medications, take him for walks, play with him, cuddle with him, groom him. Ask

Find a good kennel or pet sitter when you can't bring your Boxer with you.

about her experience with dogs and as a pet sitter. Get references and check them. Ask if she's bonded by an insurance company and whether she's affiliated with one of the national pet sitters' organizations. Find out whether she's had canine first-aid training, and discuss emergency procedures. Does she have a reliable vehicle? Can you check in with her while you're away? After you've asked all of these things, follow your instincts. Your dog will be happier at home only if the care he gets there is reliable.

Choosing your special Boxer carefully and planning ahead for his arrival in your home will pay off in many ways. You'll be more confident about your choice of breed and individual dog, and you will be more comfortable about your canine buddy fitting into your home and lifestyle. In addition, knowing how to help your pup settle in, as well as the best way to see to his well-being when you have to be away, will help you rest easier. Now it's time to enjoy your Boxer and let him enjoy you!

FEEDING
Y O U R B O X E R

You can find commercial foods for dogs from every walk of life, and hundreds of books, websites, and discussion lists that promote homemade and "natural" diets as well. And you can bet your last bit of kibble that no matter what you feed your dog, someone will be happy to tell you what's wrong with what you're feeding him.

So how can you be sure your Boxer's diet is healthful? You don't need a degree in nutrition, but three things will help keep your dog's food intake up to par. First, learn the basics of canine nutrition. Next, learn to evaluate how well your Boxer is doing on the diet he gets. Finally, if your dog develops a problem that may be food-related, such as a lack of energy, dry skin and coat, itchiness, or chronic diarrhea, be willing to look for a nutritional answer before resorting to drugs.

WHAT IS FOOD?

Dogs are carnivores, meaning that in the wild they eat mostly prey animals. Take a look at your Boxer's teeth and you'll see that they are designed for that purpose—his long canine teeth ("fangs") are designed to slash and grasp his prey, and his molars are serrated and sharp for shearing meat rather than for chewing vegetable matter. Although your dog and his wild cousins do eat and enjoy fruits and vegetables, their digestive systems are designed primarily to handle meat proteins and cannot break down the cellulose walls of vegetable matter, so raw vegetables and fruits contribute very little food value to the canine diet.

Wild carnivores eat the partly digested vegetable matter in the stomachs of their prey, who are typically herbivores with digestive systems designed to handle grass, leaves, and other vegetation. Partial digestion makes the nutrients in the vegetables available to the carnivorous hunter. Cooking does the same. Your Boxer may be a hunter at heart, but he still depends on you—or a manufacturer of high-quality dog food—to cook his veggies for him so that he can utilize the nutrients they offer. But there's a catch. Cooking destroys some vitamins in food. Good commercial dog foods have vitamins added after the heat process is completed. If you feed a homemade or raw diet, you'll probably need to include a vitamin supplement in your dog's daily rations.

Food is made up primarily of protein, fats, and carbohydrates; it also contains vitamins, minerals, some other nutrients, and water. The value of a food to a particular animal depends on that animal's nutritional needs and on how well its digestive system processes that type of food.

Proteins

Proteins are made of amino acids and are found in meat products and plants. To stay healthy, your dog needs to consume at least ten of the amino acids on a regular basis. Meat, fish, poultry, milk, cheese, yogurt, fish meal, and eggs are the best sources of complete proteins. Plants, on the other hand, provide incomplete proteins that lack some of the amino acids that dogs (and many other animals) require for optimum health. Does that mean that dogs should have a pure meat diet? No, not at all. Your dog needs vitamins and carbohydrates found in vegetables but lacking in meats.

Fats

Meats, milk, butter, and vegetable oils are also rich sources of essential fats, which insulate your Boxer against cold temperatures, help cushion his internal organs, provide energy, and help carry vitamins and other nutrients through the bloodstream to his organs. And as most of us know all too well, fat makes food taste better. Although fats are necessary in your dog's diet, they shouldn't be excessive. Some bargain dog foods are high in fat because it's cheaper than protein, and these foods may appear to provide proper nutrition for awhile because fat provides energy. Unfortunately, such foods often lack the protein, vitamins, and minerals your Boxer needs for long-term good health, and sooner or later he will show signs of chronic malnutrition.

Vitamins

Vitamins are chemical compounds that support good health in several ways. High-quality dog foods provide vitamins in the proper amounts, and fruits and the livers of most animals are also rich sources of vitamins. Heat, light, moisture, and rancidity destroy vitamins, so food should be stored properly and used before its expiration date. Although vitamins are essential for good nutrition, be cautious about supplementing your dog's diet, especially if you're feeding him a good-quality dog food. Don't give your Boxer vitamin supplements unless your veterinarian advises you to do so.

Minerals

Minerals build strong bones, strengthen cell tissue, and help organs function properly. If your dog eats a high-quality diet, he's extremely unlikely to suffer a mineral deficiency. In fact, in the US, oversupplementation is a much more common cause of health problems in dogs than is malnutrition. *Never* give your Boxer supplements containing calcium or other minerals, especially while he's growing, unless your veterinarian advises you to do so. Too much of a good thing really is too much, and you could cause serious permanent damage to your pup's growing bones and tissues.

Water

Water is also critical for life and good health. Your adult Boxer's body is about 60 percent water—as a puppy, he was even "wetter." Like other animals, your dog must maintain a balance between water in and water out. He gets much of his water by drinking, but he also uses metabolic water, or water released from food as it is digested. You may want to restrict late-night water consumption while housetraining your puppy, but otherwise your dog should have free access to clean water at all times.

FOOD, TREATS, AND SUPPLEMENTS

Now that we know what food is made of, let's take a closer look at the options available for feeding your Boxer.

Commercial Dog Foods

Venture into the pet food aisle of any pet supply, discount, or grocery store and you'll find canned foods, dry foods, and semi-moist foods. You'll see foods for puppies and senior dogs, active dogs, couch potato dogs, fat dogs,

Water is critical for your Boxer's good health.

healthy dogs, and dogs with dental problems. There are foods full of beef, chicken, turkey, lamb, duck, venison, and fish. Turn on the television, and you're sure to be bombarded with pet food ads—"Feed Wunderdogfood and your dog will look like a champion!" Obviously, all dog foods are not created equal, so it's important to know what you're buying.

Commercial dog foods are convenient, and the high-quality ones provide proper nutrition to support good canine health. Choosing a dog food strictly by price, though, could very well cost you more in the long run, both financially and emotionally. Low-quality ingredients, along with chemical preservatives and dyes used in some inexpensive foods, have been linked to serious health and behavioral problems, including cancers, allergies, and hyperactivity. Besides, quality foods may cost more per pound than poorer ones, but your dog probably eats less, making the cost per meal about the same.

What exactly is "better" about better quality dog foods? The ingredients, for one thing—many of the better foods use meats and other foods suitable for human consumption, whereas lower priced foods do not. Better foods contain less filler, so they are nutritionally more dense and therefore more digestible—no small advantage if you have pooper-scooper duty! Dogs who eat good diets also tend to be less gassy and to have healthier skin, glossier coats, cleaner, healthier teeth and gums, and better overall health.

Dry Food (Kibble)

Dry food, or kibble, comes in a wide variety of brands and qualities, and it contains a variety of ingredients. It requires no refrigeration, so it is relatively easy to store. You'll probably find that your dog's teeth and gums stay cleaner on a diet of dry kibble because the food is less likely to stick to the teeth and more likely to scrape away tartar during chewing. You can soften kibble with water if necessary, but that reduces the dental advantages of dry food. Your dog's stools will be firmer if he eats dry food; this is particularly true with high-quality dry dog foods that are more digestible and contain less filler. Dry food is generally less expensive than semi-moist and canned foods of equivalent quality.

Semi-Moist Food

There isn't much to recommend semi-moist dog foods, which basically consist of soft, kibble-like chunks. Semi-moist foods tend to cost more than dry kibble, and they tend to stick to the teeth, potentially leading to gum disease. They usually contain dyes and chemical preservatives that have been tied to health and behavioral problems in dogs. Frankly, your dog doesn't care what color his food is as long as it tastes good, so why feed him food dyes?

Canned Food

Canned, or wet, foods are comparatively expensive—after all, you have to pay for the can and the cost of shipping the water that makes the food heavy! Quality canned foods are good for dogs with certain dental or medical conditions, and they may be useful for enticing a dog whose appetite is poor due to old age or illness. However, for most dogs, a diet of canned food will probably contribute to tartar buildup, bad breath, flatulence, and soft, strong-smelling stools. Canned food also spoils quickly and must be refrigerated once opened. Insects tend to be attracted to the strong fragrance of canned dog food, so dishes must be washed soon after each meal.

Special Diets

A number of "special diets" are also available. Some are offered through conventional commercial outlets; others are sold only through veterinary clinics.

Perhaps best known are the foods aimed at owners of puppies, senior dogs, overweight dogs, and very active dogs. These are usually variations on the "adult" or "maintenance" version of the same food, with often very slight differences in nutritional content, particularly protein and fat levels, and sometimes vitamin and mineral content. Some formulas for seniors include supplements that are supposed to help fend off arthritis, and reducing formulas have fewer calories than their standard counterparts. Whether these special foods are better than a high-quality adult dog food is debatable. Many veterinarians and breeders prefer to feed adult food to puppies either from the day they begin eating solid food or from four to six months on. As for senior formulas, there's no evidence that they are better than maintenance foods for the aging dog, and supplements can be better controlled by adding them separately if needed. Reducing foods may have some value for getting weight off an obese dog quickly, but cutting back on the amount of regular adult food the dog gets will also do the trick. "Active" formula dog foods usually contain higher levels of protein and fat and can easily lead to obesity in dogs who don't need the extra calories. If you have a busy dog like a Boxer, it's easy to overestimate his nutritional needs based on his activity level. Very few dogs really are active enough to need more nutrition than is offered by proper amounts of a good adult or maintenance food.

Some special formula foods are worth the extra cost (and sometimes the trouble of finding them) for dogs with specific health problems. For instance, some dogs develop allergies to ingredients commonly used in dog foods—beef, poultry, corn, soy, and wheat in particular. Foods are available that use alternate meat sources (duck, venison, and fish are common) and replace the usual grains with oat meal, potatoes, or other vegetable sources. Other special diets are designed to support good health in dogs suffering from specific health problems such as kidney disease.

A high-quality adult or maintenance food will provide all the nutrients your active Boxer needs for proper growth.

These foods are usually available only through your veterinarian. There are also special foods that are supposed to help reduce tartar and keep your dog's teeth and gums cleaner and healthier, but before you spend the money, ask your vet about their value in maintaining your Boxer's dental health.

Homemade Diets

If, like many people, you feel that commercial diets contain questionable or inferior ingredients, you may want to consider feeding your Boxer a homemade diet. I don't mean a haphazard fare of leftovers and table scraps, mind you, but a carefully planned diet made of healthful ingredients. In fact, knowing what your dog is eating is one of the main attractions of the homemade diet. You can use high-quality meat, poultry, and fish, as well as eggs and fresh-cooked vegetables and possibly grains.

A carefully designed homemade diet can definitely provide excellent nutrition for your dog, but there are some disadvantages to homemade diets, too. You need to be sure that the food you make for your dog includes everything he needs to maintain good health. Your Boxer doesn't have to eat every single nutrient in the right amount every day, but over the course of several days, he needs to consume a proper balance of proteins, carbohydrates, fats, essential fatty acids

A carefully designed homecooked diet has many nutritional benefits, although it can have some disadvantages.

(found in fat/oils), minerals, and vitamins. This is especially critical for a growing puppy—poor nutrition during puppyhood can cause irreversible damage that will affect your dog throughout his life. If you want to make your Boxer's food, learn as much as you can about canine nutrition from reliable sources. A lot of opinions about homemade diets circulate among dog fanciers, especially on the Internet, but not all of them are based on research and facts.

Another disadvantage of a homemade diet is that it requires a fair amount of time for planning and preparation, and it requires storage space for ingredients. But if you like to cook and have the time to plan, shop, and prepare the food, as well as room to store the ingredients, then you may prefer to feed a homemade diet.

Raw Diets

Raw diets, sometimes known as Bio Active Raw Food or Biologically Appropriate Raw Food (BARF) diets, have become popular over the past 20 years. Dr. Ian Billinghurst,

Cooked bones can kill your dog. They splinter easily and can perforate your dog's intestines, causing serious injury and in many cases a painful death. Don't give your Boxer cooked bones, and keep garbage safely out of reach.

an Australian veterinarian who is the main proponent of the BARF diet, writes that dogs should eat a diet consisting of 60 percent raw meaty bones and 40 percent "a wide variety of human food scraps," mostly raw vegetables and fruits.

The bulk of the BARF diet is usually comprised of raw chicken and turkey bones, with organ meat (liver, kidney, heart, brain, tongue, and tripe) and eggs added periodically. Green leafy vegetables are included in the diet and are usually run though a food processor or juicer. Vegetable oil, brewers yeast, kelp, apple cider vinegar, fresh and dried fruits, and raw honey are often added. Some people give their dogs small portions of grain products, and some add dairy products, especially raw goat's milk, cottage cheese, and plain yogurt.

In addition to the time and storage problems mentioned earlier in regard to homemade diets, BARF-type diets pose an additional and potentially more serious challenge. Raw meat, especially raw poultry, contains bacteria that cause food poisoning, and it can also harbor parasite eggs and larva. If your Boxer enjoys good general health, his intestines will handle the bacteria without problems, although parasites can remain a threat. People, though, aren't so well equipped. For your own safety and that of your family, it's essential to keep all counter space, cutting boards, knives, plates, and storage containers scrupulously clean. It's also vital to wash your hands with soap and water after handling raw meat. Even better, wear disposable plastic gloves for the process, and wash well afterward.

Treats

Chances are your dog gets more to eat than just his meals. Most dog owners give their dogs treats for training rewards and "just because." The right kinds of treats are great in moderation and good for the souls of dogs and owners alike, but "treat abuse" isn't good for your dog. First, not all treats are created equal. It is possible to give your dog a healthful treat that he also finds yummy, but choose treats as you would a dog food. Look for small or breakable treats—you should give morsels, not mouthfuls. If you plan to use the treats for training, you want something your dog can gobble quickly so you can get back to the training, not wait around while he chews. Avoid treats that contain food dyes, and if possible, chemical preservatives.

Treats don't have to be made especially for dogs. I've trained dogs with tiny bits of raw carrots and green beans, morsels of string cheese, and itsy bits of roast chicken and deli roast beef. Plain air-popped popcorn is fine for most dogs in moderation, although some are allergic to corn. A portion of your pup's daily kibble ration can also be used for treats—you may be amazed at how yummy your dog finds regular dog food when he gets it one bit at a time.

Avoid giving your dog most human treats. He may love chips and crackers and such, but they may not like him. The grains and high fat content can cause allergic reactions, weight gain, and intestinal upsets, including flatulence and diarrhea. Your dog may also like sweets, but sugar is bad for his teeth, and chocolate is toxic for dogs. Some fruits are fine in small amounts, like little bits of apple, orange, banana, or berries, for instance, but raisins and grapes can kill a dog.

It's easy to get suckered in by those big brown eyes and the oh-so-grateful canine reaction to a handout, but even a few calories a day over his daily allotment can mean substantial weight gain even for a dog the size of a Boxer. People tend to forget the treats they hand out and can't imagine how their dogs get fat on "just this much food." But treats do add calories, and if excessive, can throw off the nutritional balance of your dog's diet. There are many more healthful ways to show your dog you love him than by overdoing the treats.

Nutritional Supplements

You can find dietary supplements that are supposed to calm your dog down, perk him up, make him shed less, give him a prettier coat, stop his itching, drive away fleas, make him grow, make him thin—you name it! Some supplements probably do help some dogs, but the claims made for many of them are at best unfounded and at worst potentially hazardous to your dog's health, not to mention your wallet.

Most dogs who are fed a balanced, healthful diet do not need supplements, and some supplements are dangerous. Excess calcium, for instance, can contribute to kidney stones and other problems in adult dogs, and in puppies can cause serious problems with bone growth that will affect the dog throughout his life. Hypervitaminosis (an excess of vitamins) is not uncommon in dogs who are given supplements, and some vitamins, especially A and D, are toxic in excessive amounts. In addition, many vitamins need to be ingested in proper ratios to other nutrients to be effective.

Your best bet is to add nutritional supplements to your puppy or dog's diet only if your veterinarian advises you to do so.

THE MECHANICS OF FEEDING YOUR BOXER

Now let's look at the nitty-gritty of feeding your Boxer, which includes how much to give him and when.

How Much Should I Feed?

The average American dog is overfed. How else can the epidemic of overweight dogs be explained? Except in very rare cases of metabolic disease, a fat dog is a dog who eats too much. In fairness to owners, most dogs will plead starvation and will eat as much as they can wheedle out of

Carefully monitor your Boxer's food intake and adjust it to meet his specific nutritional needs.

To check your dog for excess weight, place your index finger and thumb on opposite sides of the ridge of his spine over his shoulders, and run your fingers down his spine to his tail. You should be able to feel his ribs without pressing down. When you look down on your dog when he's standing, he should have a "waist" or narrowing behind his ribs. If you're not sure that he's at a proper weight, ask your vet.

people. If we consider the life of a wild canid, this opportunistic appetite makes sense; a predator never knows for sure when he'll eat his next meal, so he eats what he can when it's available. But for the well-loved pet, regular meals and food aplenty have replaced the vicissitudes of life in the wild.

The recommended portions listed on dog food packages are often considerably more than the average dog needs to maintain a healthy weight, so use them as a starting point only, and monitor your Boxer's weight and condition throughout his life. It's easy to get into a rut and continue to scoop up the same amount of food year after year, even though your dog's nutritional needs will change over time. As a growing puppy, your Boxer will need more food than he'll need as an adult, and as he ages he may need more or less food, depending on his health and activity. To maintain a healthy weight, weigh your dog at least twice a year, and evaluate the way he looks and feels.

Your dog's general health and physical appearance are the best indicators that the amount and content of your dog's diet suit him. If he's neither skinny nor fat, is alert and active as appropriate for his age, and has a glossy coat and healthy skin, then his diet is probably fine. Improper weight, lethargy, poor skin and coat, disinterest in food, changes in eating habits, and unexplained weight changes can indicate health problems, so if you notice any of these signs in your Boxer, see your vet. If your dog is healthy but picks at his food or leaves some, cut back on the amount you're giving him. If he gains or loses weight when he doesn't need to, adjust the amount of food you give him, and if his skin and coat aren't healthy but his general health checks out, consider changing his food. Don't forget to include treats when you calculate his daily consumption—those calories count, too!

Should I Schedule Meals?

There's a widespread idea that free-fed dogs—that is, dogs who have access to food all the time—won't get fat, but in fact the practice often does lead to obesity. This seems to be particularly true in multi-dog households where each dog may eat more, and more often, to beat his "competition" to the food. Scheduled feeding, in contrast, lets you control your dog's daily food intake, and therefore his weight, much more easily than free-feeding does. Scheduled feeding also makes it easier to monitor your dog's well-being. Lack of appetite is often the first sign that your dog is ill, and if you free-feed him, it may be some time before you notice that he's not eating.

Then there are the practical issues. If you're trying to housebreak a puppy or an older adoptee, free-feeding will make the process more difficult because scheduled meals make for more regular elimination, whereas a random eating schedule leads to unscheduled potty breaks. Free-feeding can also interfere with obedience training, especially if you use food treats to motivate and reward your dog. If he can eat whenever he wants to, he probably won't be as interested in training treats as he would be if food were more rare. Finally, free-feeding is impractical if you are traveling with your dog, and if you board him while you're away, he'll likely be fed on schedule, making that one more change he'll have to deal with. Another consideration, depending on where you live, is that food that's left out may attract animals and insects to your dog's bowl.

Water, of course, is a different story. The only times access to water should be limited is at night while housetraining a puppy, before anesthesia, and occasionally for other reasons as advised by your veterinarian. Otherwise, your dog should always have clean, fresh water available to drink.

The best number of meals and times to feed them depend in part on your schedule, and in part on your Boxer's age. There's no single "correct" approach to feeding. Still, some general guidelines do apply to feeding dogs at different stages in their lives.

Feeding Your Boxer Puppy

The subject of how to feed a puppy causes lots of debate among breeders, fanciers, veterinarians, and nutritionists. Some breeders specify how they want their puppies fed—a particular dog food, or a raw or homemade diet, for instance. If that's not the case for your pup, then consider the information in this book along with advice from your breeder and your veterinarian, and from other legitimate written sources, so that you can make an informed decision.

One of the hot topics is whether puppies should be fed "puppy food." Most commercial puppy foods contain extra protein and calcium to promote faster bone growth. Puppies don't need the extra nutrients, though, and larger-breed puppies like Boxers may suffer serious harm if fed too rich a diet. Extra protein and calcium cause faster bone growth, and the soft supportive tissues—tendons, ligaments, and muscles—can't grow as fast as bone. The disparity in growth rates can permanently deform the bones and rupture the connections between the tissues and bone.

If you do feed puppy food, most veterinarians and breeders recommend that you switch to adult formula when your puppy is about four months old. If you have opted to feed a raw or homemade diet, talk to your vet or a veterinary nutritionist

Never add minerals to a growing puppy's diet unless advised by your veterinarian.

about the diet you are considering. Lack of complete nutrition during the growth phase can affect your dog for his entire life, and excess amounts of some nutrients can also cause long-term damage; calcium supplements in particular are notorious for causing permanent damage to growing bones and joints. *Never* add calcium or other minerals to a growing puppy's diet unless advised to do so by your veterinarian.

Weaning practices among breeders vary quite a bit. Some "force wean" the pups sometime between four and six weeks of age, meaning that they remove the mother from the pups and feed them regular food, usually made into a "soup" initially. Other breeders allow a more natural weaning process to take place, with the puppies determining when they want to try mom's food, and letting mom decide when enough is enough with the sharp little teeth. Whichever way your pup was weaned, by six to seven weeks of age he was probably eating mostly or entirely "real" food three or four times a day, and he has learned to drink water to take the place of his mother's milk. Now it's up to you to serve up his meals.

When you pick up your puppy, your breeder should tell you what and when he's been eating, and she will probably send home a few days' worth of food as well. Keep a close eye on your puppy's growth and weight gain, and adjust his food intake as necessary to maintain growth without letting him get fat.

Again, ask your breeder's advice on feeding your Boxer. She knows her dogs. In general, puppies from 7 to 16 weeks of age need three meals a day. Their nutritional needs are high because they are growing quickly, but their stomachs are too small to hold all the food they need in just one or two feedings. Ideally, meals will be evenly spaced during your waking hours, but practically, you may need to adjust the meal schedule somewhat to fit your own work schedule. In any case, your pup needs a morning meal, a noon or afternoon meal, and an evening meal. Be sure the last meal of the day is at least a couple hours before bedtime so that your pup will eliminate before he goes to bed for the night. From 16 weeks onward, your pup needs two meals a day.

Try to feed your puppy on a regular schedule, especially while you're housetraining him. The specific times aren't important, so fit meal times into your schedule, and allow at least half an hour after the meal for pottying before you crate or confine your puppy. When your pup is older and reliably housetrained, his feeding schedule doesn't need to be quite so rigid.

Feeding Your Adolescent Boxer

For the first few months, your Boxer puppy will eat about twice as much food as he'll need as an adult, but as he approaches full growth, he'll need less food and can eat once or (preferably) twice a day. During adolescence, keep a close eye on his condition. He should show good bone and muscle development and be well covered with flesh, neither skinny nor fat. He should also be active and alert, and his coat should have a healthy shine.

Adolescence is a time of changes for dogs, as it is for people, and as we'll see later in this chapter, food can be an excellent tool for guiding your dog through this challenging training period.

Feeding Your Adult Boxer

Some people feed their adult dogs once a day, some twice. I prefer and recommend the latter—24 hours is a long time to go without a meal! Many dogs do adjust to once-a-day eating, though, so you'll need to decide what works best for you and your dog.

In any case, do keep close tabs on your Boxer's weight and condition. As he emerges from adolescence into adulthood, his metabolism will change and he may need fewer calories per day, even if he remains very active. Weigh your dog regularly if possible so that you can respond to significant weight changes quickly and effectively.

Keep in mind, too, that food is a factor in many health and behavioral problems. Food allergies, in particular, can easily go undiagnosed because they can develop over time. Your Boxer may do fine for several years on a food that contains corn, for instance, and then suddenly develop an allergic skin condition. If you suspect that food is causing your dog a problem, your veterinarian may be able to guide you. Be aware, though, that many traditional vets are not trained in nutrition and don't necessarily think of food as a factor when health problems arise. Before resorting to steroids and other drugs, consider taking your dog to a holistic vet or a veterinary allergist, or do some research of your own on food allergies and try switching your dog to a food that doesn't contain the suspected ingredient.

Feeding Your Senior Citizen Boxer

Most dog food companies now offer "light" and "senior" foods for older dogs. Usually, they contain less protein and fewer calories than maintenance foods, and some also have supplements that they claim are good for older, arthritic dogs. Although this all sounds like a great idea, there is no scientific evidence that geriatric foods offer older dogs any more benefits than a high-quality maintenance food. If your senior Boxer is healthy and in good condition, his diet is probably fine as is. There's no particular reason to change his food just because he's aging. You might want to offer him certain supplements to support aging joints and organs, but again, do so only with your vet's approval.

Some adult Boxers may need fewer calories a day than adolescents.

Older dogs sometimes become less enthusiastic about meals than they were when younger. Have you ever noticed that food doesn't taste as good when your nose is stuffy and you can't smell the aroma? The same thing may happen to your senior Boxer if his senses of smell and taste are no longer as acute as they used to be. If he seems to lose interest in his food gradually and is otherwise healthy, you may be able to pique his appetite by making his food more attractive to his old sniffer. Food is more fragrant when warm, so be sure your dog's food is room temperature or a bit warmer—but not hot! If you feed dry food, try adding a little warm water or unsalted broth a few minutes before mealtime to bring out the fragrance. Sometimes adding a little something special will make food yummier, too. A spoonful of cottage cheese, plain yogurt, or high-quality canned dog food mixed into your dog's kibble may be all that it takes to get the old guy eating again.

Untreated dental problems can also discourage your older dog from eating. Regular mouth care should be part of your Boxer's grooming routine throughout your his life, but it becomes especially important in old age. If your dog suddenly stops eating, check his teeth, gums, tongue, and the roof of his mouth for injuries or foreign objects. If his teeth are discolored or his gums look inflamed, schedule a professional teeth cleaning with your vet.

Another problem for many aging dogs is dehydration, which can contribute to serious problems. If your Boxer has trouble getting around or just doesn't feel well, he may not drink enough water. Try to keep track of how much he drinks each day, and consider making fresh water more easily available. If he spends a lot of time upstairs in the bedroom or in the basement family room, the stairs may be more trouble than a drink is worth, so think about placing an extra water bowl or two where he can get to them more easily. If your old friend has become really immobile, you might carry some water to him occasionally. Be sure to change the water in the bowl at least daily, and wash the bowl regularly to remove mineral deposits. Would you drink a glass of water that's been sitting out for a day or two? Don't ask your best friend to drink something you wouldn't drink. And again, as with lack of appetite, if you suspect that your older Boxer is not drinking properly, talk to your vet.

Elderly dogs tend to put on weight if their food intake stays the same but their activity and metabolism slow down, so in addition to good nutrition and adequate water, be sure your Boxer gets some suitable exercise as he ages. Older dogs still enjoy daily walks and reasonable games like fetch. Swimming is good exercise for old joints if your Boxer likes the water. Just don't let him swim when the water or the weather is very cold. Whatever activities he continues to pursue, don't let your dog exhaust or injure himself—he may not be willing to admit that he's no longer a youngster, and you need to protect him from himself. But as long as he's reasonably healthy, moderate activity will help your aging dog maintain muscle tone, proper weight, and a happier attitude.

CONTROLLING YOUR BOXER'S WEIGHT

Chances are that food makes your dog happy, and making him happy makes you happy—so why not show him how much you love him by feeding him what he wants? Who cares if he's a bit pudgy as long as he's happy? Hopefully, you do!

Obesity leads to serious problem in dogs, just as it does in people. Being tubby will make daily doggy life more difficult. Your dog won't be able to run as fast or jump as high without hurting himself, he'll overheat more easily, and he'll tire out more quickly. He won't even be able to curl up into a nice little doggy ball for a nap. Obesity will probably also lead to serious health problems and shorten your dog's life.

Too many pet dogs carry extra weight, and although many people claim to have no idea how their dogs got so fat, the fact is that excess weight is almost always caused by excess eating. Your dog's individual nutritional requirements are determined by several factors:

- **Activity Level.** If your dog gets a lot of running exercise, he'll need more food than if he's less active.
- **Quality of Food.** The more nutritionally dense your dog's food is and the more easily he can digest it, the less your dog needs to eat.
- **Age.** Your dog will need more food as a puppy than he'll need as an adult, and he'll need more while he's young and active than he will when he slows down later in life.

If your Boxer's lack of interest in his food persists, or if he's losing weight, take him to the vet. Loss of appetite or unexplained weight loss can indicate serious illness.

Keep an eye on your Boxer's weight as he matures, and adjust his diet if he appears to be gaining too much.

Diseases Related to Obesity

A fat dog is not a healthy dog. Obesity can lead to some serious health problems and worsen the symptoms of others, including:

- heart disease
- diabetes
- pancreatitis
- arthritis
- respiratory problems

- **Health Status.** Your dog may need more food, or specific foods, while he's recovering from an injury, surgery, or illness than he does at other times.
- **Individual Variation.** Your dog's individual nutritional needs, and his response to environmental factors that affect those needs, are his and his alone. Two Boxers of the same age and lifestyle may need different amounts of food to maintain a healthy weight. Even two pups from the same litter may have very different nutritional needs.

Ideally, your Boxer will carry the proper amount of weight from puppyhood through old age, but sometimes extra padding sneaks on before we notice. (Believe me, I know!) If your pup turns pudgy, don't despair—you can do a number of things to get him back in shape.

First, measure his meals using a standard measuring device. It's awfully easy to get into the habit of scooping "one serving" without realizing that your scoop is closer to two servings. Keep track, too, of the treats your dog gets during the day. If you're not sure, try measuring out treats for the day and limit your dog to those. (Be sure other family members follow this system, too.) You might even set aside part of your dog's regular daily portions to use as treats. Your buddy will think the food is special when handed out piecemeal, and the "treats" won't add calories to his diet.

If your Boxer needs to lose weight, you can simply cut back on the amount you feed, of course. But if that makes you feel bad, there are a few tricks you can use. If you feed dry dog food, soak a quarter of the meal in water until it's soft—the soaked pieces will expand and be more filling. At mealtime, mix half his regular dry portion with the soaked food and serve. Your dog will eat a fourth less food, but it will seem like more. Another doggy diet trick is to cut back on your dog's regular food and add low-calorie, high-fiber food to his diet. Some popular choices are unsalted green beans (fresh are fine), shredded or sliced carrot, lettuce or spinach, canned pumpkin (not pie filling, just pumpkin), or unsalted, air-popped popcorn (unless he's allergic to corn). He may look at you as if you've lost your mind the first few meals, but most dogs eventually realize that this odd stuff really is food, and it tastes pretty good to boot. If none of those tactics work, ask your vet about a weight-loss or lower calorie food.

Some people think that a dog with the high energy level of a Boxer will naturally stay slim. Don't count on it; I've seen more than a few pudgy Boxers! Adjust your dog's diet as necessary to keep him at an appropriate weight. He'll live a longer, healthier, happier life, and he'll look a lot better, too.

THE SOCIAL SIDE OF FOOD

Most people realize that there is a profoundly social aspect to food and meals among our own species. The same is true for dogs. The most basic social principal related to food as it relates to dogs is that control of food signals social dominance. This simple fact can work to a dog owner's great advantage if understood and used properly, or it can lead to serious problems if improperly managed.

The Golden Rule of Food Management

There's an old adage that defines the Golden Rule thus: "He who has the gold rules." We can apply the same principal to our relationship with our dogs, changing "gold" to "food." One of the most common—and most dangerous—problem behaviors seen in Boxers and other dogs is what behaviorists call resource guarding, which is an animal's attempt to keep a resource to himself.

Food is a resource, and your dog may try to exert some control over his food by guarding it, especially from other animals and children. If allowed to continue, the behavior escalates to outright threats, and potentially, bites. In my house, resource guarding by dogs is simply not allowed, especially if people are involved. For more on preventing and stopping resource guarding, see Chapter 6.

Beggars Can Be Learners

Most dogs are born with a begging gene, and most people who like dogs are easy targets. Fortunately, dogs are also born with an implicit understanding that life isn't fair and doesn't always give them what they want. It's your job to teach your dog two important lessons that work together. First, he needs to learn that staring and begging won't get you to hand over your food. You can teach this by never, ever rewarding your dog for begging. If begging never works, he'll stop doing it. This is a case in which "never" really does mean *never*—an occasional bit of food when your dog is being a pest will make him even more persistent next time. This rule applies whether you're snacking on the sofa or eating dinner at the table. I would also recommend that you teach your dog to lie down on the floor whenever you or anyone else is eating so that minding his own business becomes a habit.

If you want to share a little tidbit with your buddy once in a while, that's okay. (Just don't fatten him up on treats!) Wait until you've finished eating, then take your dog to another area, have him do something, like an obedience command or a trick, and then give him a teensy taste. In fact, as we'll see in Chapter 6, food can be used as a highly motivating reward. Your Boxer can't work for money, but he can learn to "work" for food, and he'll be a better, happier companion for it.

There's no question that food makes the dog. In fact, good nutrition enables your Boxer to grow and develop properly as a puppy and adolescent. It keeps him healthy and fit and promotes mental and emotional health throughout his life. It also helps him to live longer and remain active into his senior years while enhancing his life as a member of a social group. Indeed, the theme song of many dogs would be, I think, "Food, glorious food!"

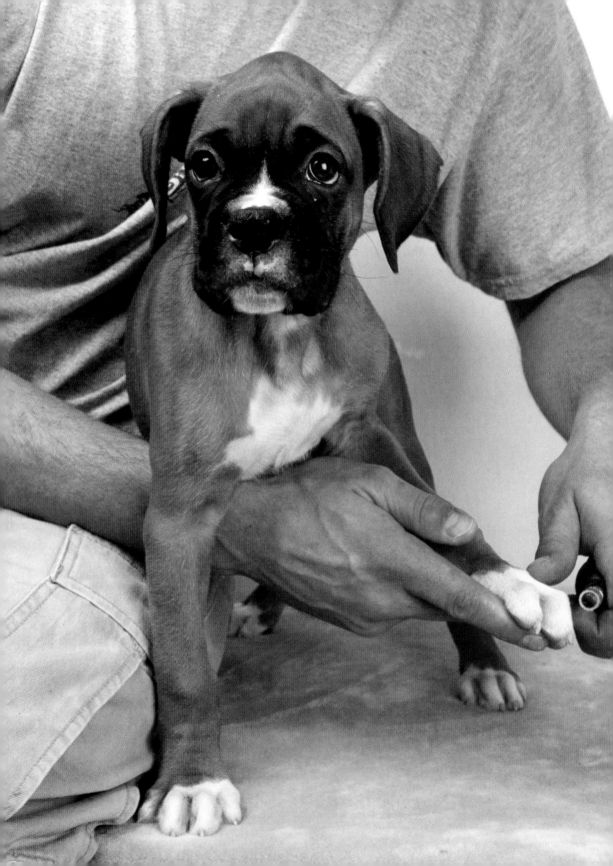

GROOMING
YOUR BOXER

Y ou've probably heard that Boxers don't need much grooming. It is true that they don't require hours of brushing or trimming like some dogs, but grooming is still an important part of having a Boxer.

WHY SHOULD YOU GROOM YOUR BOXER?

Okay, so why bother grooming a dog who's pretty much wash-and-wear? For one thing, grooming sessions are special times for you and your dog. If you're gentle, and if you talk to your dog while you groom, he'll learn to love the feel of your hands on his body just as you love the feel of his warm fur against your skin. He'll also learn to trust your hands, which is very important in training and in an emergency. Happily, many owners also find grooming sessions to be relaxing, almost therapeutically pleasant times if the dog has been taught to accept and enjoy the process.

There are benefits from grooming for your Boxer's health, too. Obviously, regular grooming sessions keep him cleaner, but they also give you a chance to check him for cuts, bites, bumps, sore spots, and other early signs of health problems that you might not otherwise notice until they become serious.

Regular grooming also helps to minimize the additional housework that's part of living with a dog. Brushing removes loose hair that would otherwise end up on your furniture, floors, carpets, and clothes, and trimming nails makes them less likely to scratch floors or snag carpets or upholstery. All in all, grooming is a very good thing even for a low-maintenance dog like the Boxer.

COAT CARE

Your Boxer's smooth, sleek coat is pretty much wash-and-wear, but to look and feel his best your dog will still need some coat care.

Since Boxers are a short-coated breed and are fairly clean themselves, they rarely need baths. Boxers do shed, but dead hair can be removed easily with a weekly brushing with a bristle brush and a curry comb in fall and spring when shedding is heavier.

Brushing

To remove loose hairs and dirt from your Boxer's coat, use a rubber curry comb in a circular

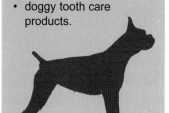

motion. Most dogs enjoy a vigorous massage with the curry, but be gentle where the bone is less well padded. You can then smooth the coat back down and give it a last-minute polish with a soft bristle brush.

If you suspect your dog has unwanted passengers, like fleas, use a flea comb to comb through the coat. The narrow spaces between the teeth will catch any fleas that are present and alert you to a possible flea problem before it gets out of hand.

Splish Splash, I Was Taking a Bath!

Most Boxers don't need to be bathed very often, but you'll probably want to bathe your dog occasionally—more often if he's a real outdoor type who likes to indulge in the popular doggy pastime of rolling in stinky stuff! Many people and dogs alike approach doggy bath time reluctantly,

Your Boxer's smooth, sleek coat is easy to take care of with weekly brushings.

but it doesn't have to be a test of wills and reflexes if you take the time to teach your dog that the tub or sink is a safe and not-so-unpleasant place.

Begin bath training as soon as you get your dog, and (hopefully) before you need to bathe him. Put your pup in the tub or sink, give him a treat, praise him, and pet him gently. If he struggles to get out, hold him there firmly but gently and talk to him quietly. When he stops struggling, take him out of the tub. Don't reward him or make a fuss over him after he's out! You want him to learn that he gets rewards for being in the tub, not for getting out. Repeat this process once or twice a day for a while, slowly increasing the time he has to stay in the tub. When he's comfortable in the dry tub, add a little lukewarm water so he gets his feet wet, and continue to reward him. When he accepts the "wet feet routine," wet his body with lukewarm water from a sprayer or by pouring water onto him from an unbreakable container, again rewarding him for accepting it. Like all training, this approach takes some planning and time, but you'll end up with a dog who accepts bath time without fear and who may even enjoy being bathed. Now he's ready for a real bath!

Before you begin, make sure everything you need is close by, as you can't exactly ask your soapy dog to wait in the tub while you run downstairs for towels. Here's what you need:
- Dog shampoo
- Cotton balls
- Ophthalmic ointment
- Nonslip mat
- A hose or unbreakable container for rinsing
- One or two towels
- Hair catcher for the drain

First, brush your dog to remove loose hair. Place a cotton ball into the opening of each ear to protect the ear canal against water, but don't push it in too far. Apply an ophthalmic ointment (available from your vet, groomer, or pet supply store) to the eyes to protect them from soap burns, or be *very careful* not to get soap into his eyes. (Rinse thoroughly if you do.) Next, put your dog into the tub or sink, and reward him as you did in training.

Wet your dog with lukewarm water, then apply shampoo and work it in with your fingers, beginning at your dog's neck and working toward the tail. Don't forget his belly, up under the hind legs, and under his tail. And here's a little trick—you can save money and make lathering and rinsing easier if you dilute your dog's shampoo before you apply it rather than after. Mix one part shampoo with one or two parts water in a clean squirt bottle, shake well, and apply a small amount of the mixture to your dog. Don't lather your dog's face; use a washcloth for more control, and don't get shampoo in his eyes.

A word about shampoos: Shampoo for people will dry and damage your dog's skin and coat, so use shampoo formulated for dogs. Special shampoos are available for certain skin conditions, but unless your vet recommends one, all you need is a good quality, mild doggy shampoo. If you're trying to kill fleas, you don't need insecticidal shampoo. Using regular dog shampoo, wet and lather your dog thoroughly, beginning with a "collar" of lather high on his neck to keep any fleas leaving his body from hiding in his ears. Leave the lather on for about ten minutes to drown the fleas, then rinse.

Rinsing is as important as any other part of the bath. Be sure to rinse thoroughly, because soap residue can cause skin irritation. Go over your dog's body with your hands after rinsing to be sure you got all the soap, and pay particular attention to his armpits, under his hind legs, and the groove along his belly between his ribs where soap loves to hide. When you're sure all the soap is out, gently squeeze the excess water from your dog's coat. Then rub him vigorously with a towel, finishing up by smoothing his fur in the direction of growth.

Be sure to praise and reward your dog for being so good before you release him, then *carefully* let him go so that he doesn't hurt himself or something else with a wild leap. With many dogs it's a good idea to put a collar and leash on before letting go. "Crazy dog attacks" are common after baths, and most dogs like to run and roll and rub themselves on things (like carpets, walls, furniture, bedspreads). You might want to confine your dog to a particular room or his crate until he's dry, and be sure to keep him warm and out of drafts. If he needs to go out, take him on leash—wet dogs love nothing better than to roll in the dirt! You can blow dry your dog if you like, but don't use a hot setting, as it will dry out his skin and coat.

Before using any grooming or flea-prevention products on a puppy or a dog with health problems, be sure to read all instructions and warning labels. Better yet, ask your vet. Some products are dangerous for puppies or for dogs with health problems.

HEALTHY FEET AND NAILS

We all know how painful it is to walk on sore feet. The same applies to your dog, especially if he's very active or spends a lot of time outdoors. Check his feet frequently, particularly between his toes and pads where burrs, stones, small sticks, and other debris can get stuck. Remove foreign matter carefully with your fingers or tweezers.

Keep your Boxer's nails trimmed short. Long nails that

To maintain the health of your Boxer's feet, keep his nails trimmed short.

hit·the ground force the toes out of their normal position, distorting the foot and potentially causing lameness and permanent deformity. If you hear the click of nails when your dog walks on a hard surface, it's time for a pedicure.

Nail trimming needn't be difficult, and there are some things you can do to keep it that way. If you touch your dog's feet only to clip his nails, he'll probably object, so you need to teach him that having his feet handled is no big deal. When you're relaxing together, hold each of your pup's feet one at a time, gently massaging and flexing his toes. Start with short sessions. If he objects, hold one foot gently and give him a treat *while still holding his foot*. Be sure you reward him for letting you hold his foot, not for pulling it away. Do this for a few sessions without trying to trim his nails. When he's comfortable with having his feet held, try trimming one nail. If he doesn't fight you, great! But if he's not yet sure about this, trim just one nail, and give him a treat while you're still holding his foot, then let go. Do another nail later. Be sure to continue paw-holding sessions without trimming, too. Before you know it you'll be trimming all his nails in one session without frightening or fighting with your dog.

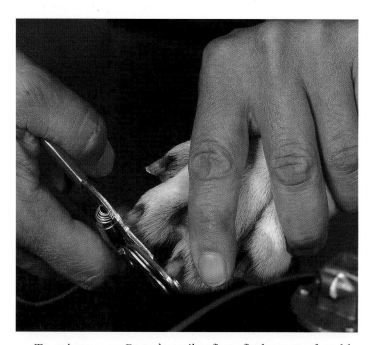

Be careful not to cut your Boxer's nails too close to the quick.

To trim your Boxer's nails, first find a comfortable position and be sure you have sufficient light. You might have your Boxer lie on your lap or have him stand, sit, or lie on a grooming table or on a towel on a table at a height that's comfortable for you. Hold his paw gently but firmly. Press gently on the bottom of the footpad to extend the nail, and trim the nail below the quick. If your dog has light-colored nails, the quick will look pink from the blood vessels inside it. If his nails are dark, cut below the place where the nail narrows and curves downward. Trim the tip, and then look at the end of the nail. If you see a black dot near the center of the nail, you're at the quick and it's time to stop trimming. If not, you can shave a little more off. Don't forget the dewclaws, those funny little toes located on the insides of the legs above the front feet.

If you accidentally cut the quick, put a little styptic powder (available from pet supply or drug stores) or corn starch into the palm of your hand or a shallow dish and dip the nail into it. The powder will stick to the nail and seal the blood vessel. Clippers leave sharp, rough edges, but you can smooth them out with a few short, downward strokes of an emory board. (The ones made for acrylic nails work well on doggy nails.)

Be sure your nail clippers are sharp and working well. Dull or poorly aligned blades won't cut cleanly, and they may pinch, which won't make your dog like nail trimming time any better! If you're still not sure how to trim the nails, have your veterinarian show you the proper angle and length. As a last resort, you can have them done at the vet's office or by a groomer, but please don't wait for your dog's annual exam to get his nails trimmed. They should be done every three to six weeks, depending on your individual dog.

EAR CARE

Ear problems aren't as common in Boxers as they are in some breeds, but they do occur. Allergies, hormonal problems, and excess moisture can all promote abnormal growth of yeast or bacteria in the moist, warm ear canal. Ear mites are not as common in dogs as they are in cats, but if your Boxer has mites and is sensitive to mite saliva, he may go nuts and even hurt himself scratching his itchy ears. A playful Boxer can also get dirt, plant matter, or other things in his ear, causing him to scratch and possibly injure his ear.

Check your Boxer's ears once a week by looking at and sniffing them. The skin inside his ear should be pink or flesh colored and should not look red or inflamed. You may see a little wax, but it shouldn't be excessive, and you shouldn't see dirty-looking discharge, nor should you smell any strong or nasty odors. Even if you can't see or smell anything amiss, your dog may have a problem if he's persistently scratching or rubbing at his ears or head, shaking or tilting his head, or crying or pulling away when you touch his ears or the area around them.

Don't try to treat ear problems without veterinary advice. Ear infections are painful and can cause permanent hearing loss. Effective treatment requires accurate diagnosis, and treating your dog with an inappropriate over-the-counter or homemade remedy will prolong your dog's discomfort. It may also cause more damage and make the infection more difficult to treat later.

If your dog's ears are dirty but not inflamed or sensitive, clean them with a commercial or homemade ear cleaner. Take your dog outdoors or to a bathroom or other area where cleanup will be easy—ear cleaning can get messy. Squirt plenty of cleaner into the ear to flush it out, then push the ear flap over the opening of the ear and massage for a few seconds to work the cleaner into the ear canal. Then let go and stand back! Your dog will shake his head and throw cleaner and whatever it flushes far and wide. When both ears are cleaned and shaken, gently wipe your dog's ears out with a cotton ball or tissue. *Never* push anything into your dog's ear canals. If your Boxer seems to have very waxy ears or if he plays in water frequently, clean his ears about once a week. If his ears stay nice and clean on their own, you don't need to do anything except check them regularly.

EYE CARE

One of the most appealing parts of a Boxer are his beautiful, expressive eyes. However, because the Boxer's eyes protrude slightly, they are prone to injury. This means you need to use extra caution and see your vet if your dog's eyes seem irritated. Healthy doggy eyes are clear and moist, with no sign of redness, swelling, excess tearing, mucus, or squinting, any of which can indicate infection, abrasion, or other problems. If you notice any of these symptoms, take your dog to the vet.

Routine canine eye care is pretty simple. Some mucus at the inner corners of the eyes is normal, but if it builds up, the mucus can harbor bacteria that may cause an eye infection. This is why if you see that your dog has "eye gunk," you should gently wipe it away with a moist washcloth or tissue. You can also protect your dog's eyes from injury by using good sense when he travels. The image of a dog riding along with the wind in his face may be appealing, but even a tiny insect or bit of dirt hitting an eye at the speed of a moving vehicle can cause serious injury. Keep your Boxer away from open windows, or better yet, have him travel safely in a crate. Be careful, too, when bathing your dog or applying any products on his face—soap and chemicals can cause serious eye damage, including blindness.

As your dog gets older, you may notice a cloudiness in his eyes. Often this is nuclear sclerosis, a change in the lens associated with aging. Unless severe, it usually causes no vision problems. Clouding may, however, indicate a cataract, which can affect vision. Talk to your veterinarian about changes in your dog's eyes.

DENTAL CARE

Although cavities are rare in dogs who eat normal canine diets (no sugary treats!), gum disease is very common in adult dogs. Bacteria from unhealthy gums can contribute to heart, liver, and kidney disease, cause "dog breath," and lead to tooth loss. Although the idea of regular doggy dental care may seem daunting, it's really no more complicated than it is for us. It's just a matter of training your dog to accept it as part of regular grooming and training yourself to stick with the program.

The first step is to establish a regular at-home dental care regime for your Boxer. Bacteria and food particles collect along the gum line and form plaque, which will turn to tartar (calculus) and irritate the gums, leading to gingivitis (inflammation of the gum). If tartar builds up under the

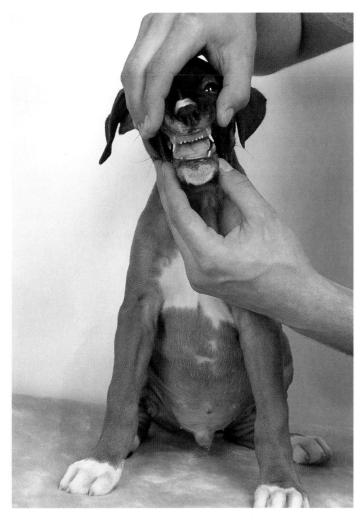

The first step in a good dental care program is to establish regular at-home dental checks.

gums, it causes periodontal disease, resulting in abscesses, infection, and loss of teeth and bone. Ideally, your dog should have his teeth brushed every day to remove the plaque, but even every few days will go a long way toward preventing tartar from forming.

Your vet can teach you to brush your dog's teeth properly and can recommend toothbrushes, plaque removers, and toothpastes that are safe for use on dogs. Toothbrushes for dogs are smaller, softer, and shaped differently than ours. Many people prefer to use a dental sponge, which is a small disposable sponge with a flexible handle. If your dog's gums are sensitive, or if you have difficulty managing his toothbrush, you can wrap surgical gauze around your finger, dampen it with water, dip it in a little canine toothpaste or baking soda, and rub it over your dog's teeth and gums.

In addition to regular home dental care, your Boxer should have dental checkups as part of his routine veterinary care. Your vet will check your dog's teeth and mouth and recommend thorough cleaning and polishing under anesthesia once or twice a year. If your pup develops bad breath, visible tartar along the gum line, bleeding gums, or other oral problems between checkups, take him to your vet.

A diet of high-quality dry dog food can help slow the formation of plaque, and some companies now offer special foods that are supposed to help prevent plaque. Nylabone chew toys and dental devices, as well as raw or sterilized beef bones, may also help.

If you have a puppy, check his mouth and teeth every few days. Puppies, like human babies, are born toothless. Their deciduous, or baby, teeth begin to come in at about four weeks. The baby teeth are then replaced by permanent teeth when the puppy is between three and five months old. Occasionally a baby tooth isn't pushed out properly by the permanent tooth. Such retained deciduous teeth are most commonly incisors or upper canines ("fangs"). Retained deciduous teeth will cause the permanent teeth to be misaligned and keep the jawbones from developing properly, leading to pain, difficulty eating, and other problems. If you suspect that your Boxer pup has retained a baby tooth, take him to your vet.

ANAL SAC CARE

Ever wonder why dogs sniff each others' fannies when they meet and greet one another? Like other predators, your dog has anal sacs (anal glands) located on both sides and slightly below his anus that produce an odor that identifies him to other dogs. In a healthy dog, the anal glands express, or empty, themselves onto the surface of the stool every time the dog has a bowel movement, which is why dogs find poop so fascinating. It tells them who else has passed their way.

If the anal glands fail to empty regularly, they can become impacted. Impacted glands are not dangerous in themselves, but they are uncomfortable and can cause an affected dog to bite at the area or scoot along the floor, potentially injuring the delicate tissue surrounding his anus. They can also make defecation difficult or painful and can lead to a painful infection or abscess. In some cases, the impaction can be relieved by manually expressing, or cleaning out, the anal glands. The odor of anal gland fluid isn't appealing to people as it is to dogs, but if you're brave, you can have your vet or groomer teach you how to express the glands. If that doesn't sound like a skill you want to master, you can have your vet or groomer do the job when necessary. Chronically impacted anal glands can be relieved in some cases by feeding the dog a high-fiber diet, causing bulkier stools that express the glands when they pass. The anal glands can also be removed in serious cases.

CHOOSING A PROFESSIONAL GROOMER

Although your Boxer doesn't need a lot of grooming, there may be times when he needs to be groomed and you'd rather not do it yourself. That's when you need a professional groomer. To find a good, reliable groomer, ask your veterinarian, family, and friends for recommendations. Most groomers are kind and gentle with dogs, but as in any business, there are unfortunate exceptions. Here are some questions to ask:

- What training and experience do the groomers in the shop have?
- Are they used to handling large, strong dogs?
- What kind of shampoos and conditioners do they use?
- What other products do they use on your breed?
- Do they use a hand-held drier or cage drier? If a cage drier, how often do they check your dog? Is someone always present when the dog is exposed to the drier?
- Do they clean the ears?
- Do they check, and if necessary, express the anal glands?
- Do they use sedatives? If so, who sedates and monitors the pet? What training have they had in the safe use of sedatives and in first aid? What will they do if something goes wrong?
- How long will your dog need to be there? Where will he be kept when he's not being groomed? Where will he be taken to potty? Is the area fenced?
- What are the normal fees for a Boxer, and what is included in that fee?

The facilities should be tidy and clean, and dogs who aren't being groomed should be housed in secure, reasonably comfortable cages or crates with access to drinking water. Equipment, like scissors, combs, brushes, clippers, and grooming tables, should be disinfected between dogs. If you don't feel comfortable about a groomer, don't leave your dog with that establishment. Trust your instincts, and don't be polite at the expense of your peace of mind or your dog's well-being.

Compared to many other breeds, Boxers need so little grooming that it's easy to forget they need any at all. But there are, as we've seen, good reasons to groom your Boxer regularly. Brushing keeps him clean and gives you an opportunity to check him for lumps, bumps, and parasites. Tooth care will keep his pearlies nice and white and alert you to any oral problems. Nail trimming will keep his feet healthy, and regular ear care will prevent infections from setting in. The occasional bath will spiff him up when necessary. And in addition to all of these benefits, the time you spend together grooming can be an opportunity to strengthen your relationship.

Don't use toothpaste made for people on your Boxer's teeth—it can cause stomach distress when swallowed, and few people can teach their dogs to rinse and spit!

TRAINING AND BEHAVIOR

OF YOUR BOXER

Do you remember when we discussed the Boxer's heritage as a working dog? That information will be important as you train your Boxer, because the characteristics for which he was developed—confidence, strength, intelligence, and loyalty—affect your dog's behavior and his responses to training. Boxers are very trainable, but like all intelligent, high-energy dogs, they need to be trained in a way that motivates them to learn. Your Boxer will get bored easily, so you need to make training fun and interesting for him. Although all training should be done with kindness and respect for your dog, it's also important that your Boxer learns to respect you. In fact, knowing that you're in control of the situation will make life and learning easier for your dog. Let's start with some basic information about dog training and then talk about some specifics.

BEFORE YOU TRAIN

Many people think of their dogs as "fur people" who have more hair and more legs than we do but who otherwise are pretty much like us. But dogs are much more interesting if we see them for what they are—another species that has lived with us for thousands of years, developing its own strengths and wagging its way into human lives and emotions while remaining true to its canine heart.

Almost everything your Boxer does is either instinctive or learned. (The exceptions would be behaviors that result from outside influences such as illness, injury, or chemicals.) The most effective way to direct your dog's behavior and to prevent and deal with problem behaviors is to learn about normal canine behavior and instincts and use that knowledge to your advantage. With understanding and planning, you can teach your dog what you want and don't want from him. You can also prevent many potential problem behaviors and put an end to others. Your Boxer will quickly learn to understand *your* behavior and use it to his advantage, and there's no reason you can't reciprocate.

Why Train Your Boxer?

Although the benefits of a trained dog may be self-evident to us humans, they aren't necessarily so obvious to the dog. Boxers are intelligent dogs, developed to work closely with people, which makes them relatively easy to train compared to some breeds. But it's important to understand that motivation, not intelligence, is what makes a dog trainable, or more precisely, makes him willing to be trained. Boxers do want to please their people, but they are also self-serving, as are all dogs. In other words, in order to teach your dog to behave in ways that please you, you need to help him see what's in it for him.

Training is basically the process of teaching your dog new habits that you want him to have. Keep in mind that your Boxer is always learning, whether you think you're training him or not. If he does something successfully more than two or three times, it's likely to become a habit. This means your job is to prevent him from repeating behaviors you don't want and teach him behaviors that you do want. Rather than saying, "No!" all the time, try saying, "Do this instead." It's much easier to promote good habits than to change bad ones once they're established.

His intelligence and independence make your Boxer a more challenging dog to train than some because he's easily bored by repetition. Letting him train himself will probably create a monster, but holding up your side of the canine-human bargain by providing an education will help him become a terrific companion. If you're creative and consistent, and if you use positive motivational training methods and offer your dog activities that engage his agile mind, training your Boxer can be rewarding for both of you.

Seven Secrets of Success

Regardless of what you're teaching your dog, there are seven principles that always apply. It isn't always easy to stick to them, but if you manage to most of the time, these tips will help you train successfully:

1. **Be Consistent.** Use one word and/or signal to mean one thing. Your Boxer is not a native speaker of human language. He'll learn "sit" without much trouble, but "baby, please sit here by me" or "you better sit right now!" or "sit...sit down!" will be so much gibberish. Similarly, don't say "down" to mean "lie down" one time and "don't jump up" the next. Use different commands for different actions.

2. **Be Concise.** Tell him something only once. If you repeat a command, your Boxer will quickly learn that he doesn't have to respond until you say, "Come...come....come.... come" or yell or jump up and down or otherwise indicate that now you really mean come.

3. **Be Generous.** Reward your dog for responding correctly. While it may be obvious to you that coming when you call is desirable, it may not be so obvious to your dog, especially if there are good smells to check out or squirrels to chase. This is why it's important to apply the principles of positive motivation discussed later in this chapter.

4. **Be Smart.** Don't tell your Boxer to do something if you can't make him do it. You should teach your dog that he must do what you say when you say it, and if you're a smart trainer, you'll end up with a reliable dog. So if you want your Boxer to come when you call him, don't try to call your dog in from the yard when you're dripping wet and wrapped in a towel unless you're willing to go get him anyway!

5. **Be Prepared.** If you need a long line for control when you call your dog to come in, then keep the long line by the back door and put it on him when he goes out so you can reel him in if he doesn't come when called.

6. **Be Cheerful.** This is your friend you're talking to! Dogs respond to happy voices, so

sound happy when you give commands and when you praise. Even if he doesn't understand all the words, your Boxer will certainly understand your tone.

7. **Be Nonviolent.** Never, ever hit your dog. Hitting doesn't teach your Boxer what you want him to do, but it does teach him that you can't be trusted.

What Do You Want Your Boxer to Know?

Before you start training—and better yet, before you bring your Boxer home—you need to decide what it is you want him to know. Will you be happy if he learns simply to be well mannered in the house and on walks? Or do you plan to pursue more advanced training for competition or other activities? Your long-term goals will affect where and how you train your dog.

Whether you're aiming simply for a well-mannered pet or you're planning to go on to higher levels of training, encourage all human members of your household to follow the same rules and use the same words and methods for teaching and reinforcing behaviors. Be forewarned, though, that family and friends are a lot harder to train than Boxers are!

The Power of Positive Reinforcement

Your goal right from the start in training should be to forge a bond of trust, mutual respect, and understanding with your dog. If you also teach him that learning is fun, training at all levels will progress more quickly and you and your Boxer will enjoy each other more. The most effective and fair way to forge such a bond is through positive reinforcement.

Positive reinforcement is the process of rewarding your dog for doing what you want him to do. The reward has to be something that your dog likes and wants—for many dogs, food is highly motivating, but toys, petting, and even a chance to run in circles can all be rewards if the individual dog is motivated to work for them. It's your job to figure out what really motivates your individual Boxer.

Training Tools

Having the right equipment can make training your dog easier and more effective. The toughest part is deciding what's right!

Collar

Ask three dog trainers what kind of collar or leash is "best" and you're likely to get three different suggestions.

One effective collar for training is a flat collar made of leather, nylon, or fabric that closes with a buckle or a quick-release fastener. This is the type of collar that should carry your dog's name, license, and rabies tags. You should be able to slide two fingers between the fastened collar and your dog's neck. If you train with a flat collar, it should not have tags attached, so you might need one for training, one for the rest of the time. The only downside to flat collars is that they don't provide much control, and some dogs can slip out of them. However, for some types of training, it's a good choice. The only collar that should be used on the delicate neck of a young puppy is a flat collar.

You can positively train your Boxer using food rewards.

Choke chains are usually made of metal links, but they also come in nylon and leather. Although many good dog trainers use choke chains without hurting their dogs, people frequently misuse these collars, making them at best ineffective for training and control and at worst dangerous to the dog's neck and throat.

A halter (or head collar) looks something like a horse halter and controls the dog by controlling his head. Halters are very effective for control—so much so that people who use them often control but do not train their dogs, ending up with a dog they can't control unless he's wearing a halter. If you decide to try a halter on your Boxer, be sure to get one made specifically for brachycephalic dogs, and have a knowledgeable trainer fit it properly to your dog.

Leash

You will also need at least one leash. Most experienced trainers prefer leather leashes because they are easy on the hands, and they give you and your dog a good feel for one another's movements. The length of the leash depends on your height and preferences. For a Boxer, you will probably want a 4- to 6-foot long leash $3/4$ of an inch to 1 inch wide.

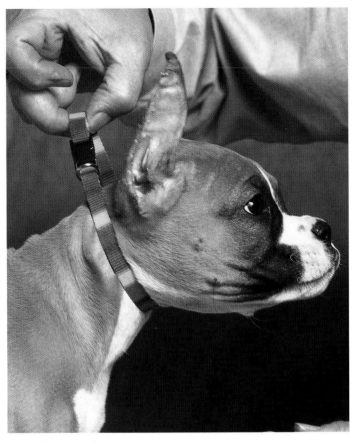

Find a proper leash and collar before you start training your Boxer.

Training Words

In addition to specific commands, you need to teach your dog two special training words. Your praise word will tell your dog when he's correct. In the beginning, say the word as you give your dog his reward—food or play. He'll soon come to value the praise itself, because it's been associated with good things. Find a word your dog doesn't hear all the time; if you're always telling your dog he's a "good boy" just for lying on the couch, don't use "good boy" for praise in training. I use "excellent" to praise my dogs. Your release word will tell your dog that he no longer has to perform the behavior—he sat when you told him to, and now he doesn't have to sit. Many people use "okay," but I recommend that you use a word your dog doesn't hear all the time so you don't accidentally release him. I use "free!" to release my dogs.

Voice, Body Language, and Attitude

The final absolutely essential training tools you already have: your voice, body, and attitude. You can use your voice, body language, and attitude to communicate with your dog. Dogs respond much better to a happy sounding voice than to grumbles and growls, so pay attention to the tone of your commands, praise, and corrections. Dogs are also very attuned to posture and movement, so try to be relaxed and confident rather than tense or uncertain when you train.

STARTING OUT ON THE RIGHT PAW

Start training your Boxer as soon as you bring him home. Whether he's a puppy or an adult, he will need to learn the rules and routine of your home. Your Boxer is smart, but he can't read your mind. What he *can* do is learn what he needs to know to make you the happiest dog owner in town. Nothing you buy for your pup will mean a thing if you can't live with him, so give him—and yourself—an education.

Establishing Household Rules

Decide on the rules before you bring your Boxer home, and be sure that everyone in the household knows what they are. If you're getting a puppy, think ahead to how you want him to behave as an adult. It's confusing and unfair to allow a puppy special privileges and remove them later. If anything, he should gain privileges as he matures. So if you don't want your adult Boxer sleeping on the bed, don't let him sleep there as a puppy. The same goes for basic good manners. If you don't want your adult Boxer to jump up on you and other people, don't let him do it as an adorable baby. If you don't want him to stare at you and drool when you're eating when he's grown, don't give him handouts while he's young. We all know that bad habits are hard to break, so be careful about the habits you encourage in your new dog.

Training goes on all the time, so take advantage of opportunities throughout the day to teach and reinforce the behaviors you want in your dog. In addition, plan two or three short training sessions in which you focus on one or two behaviors. Puppies have very short attention spans, but they learn very quickly. This means that several five-minute training sessions on basic lessons such as sit, come, and down can be very productive. Older Boxers can focus longer, but they're easily bored by repetition, so as your dog matures you can train for longer periods. However, don't focus on one thing for more than five or ten minutes, and if he does it right, don't keep repeating it in that session.

The Importance of Socialization

Socialization is the process of making your puppy familiar with the world around him and its inhabitants. Puppies and adolescent dogs need to meet all kinds of people: old, young, male, female, different races, bearded and clean-shaven. Puppies also need to meet other nonaggressive dogs and experience as many sights and sounds as you can provide. Exposure to this wide variety of people, places, and things will make your adult dog more confident and comfortable throughout his life.

Socialization with people is particularly important when your pup is between 7 and 14 weeks old, but the process should continue throughout puberty and young adulthood. During adolescence, when your dog is 12 to 18 months old, he may lose some of his manners and flex his muscles a bit, possibly challenging some members of the household for higher rank in the

It's important to socialize your Boxer to all types of people, children, and other dogs.

"pack" to which he belongs. Think of him as a canine teenager and his behavior will make more sense. During this time, gentle but firm and consistent reinforcement of household manners and rules will help the human members of your household keep their socially superior positions in your dog's eyes. If your Boxer has already completed an obedience class, this is a great time to take another. If he hasn't yet been to doggy school, it's definitely time to sign him up!

Crate Training

A crate is an essential tool for training your puppy or new dog, keeping him and your belongings safe, and keeping your sanity as your new Boxer masters the rules of responsible doggy adulthood. If you use the crate as it's meant to be used, your dog will consider it his den and may even choose to go there on his own at times.

When he's first learning to be in his crate, your Boxer may complain. Don't give in to his whining, barking, or howling—if you let him out, he will quickly learn that noise is his ticket to freedom. Grit your teeth until he gets quiet (he will eventually) and then reward him either with a treat in the crate or by letting him out. Don't let him out and then give him a treat or he'll think you're rewarding him for getting out of the crate!

Choose a crate that is big enough for your Boxer to stand up, turn around, and lie down in. An adult Boxer needs a crate approximately 24 inches wide by 36 inches long by 28 inches high, but if you're housetraining a puppy, you may want to use a smaller crate than your dog will need as an adult. You can even block off part an adult-size crate to limit the usable space. Healthy dogs raised in clean surroundings don't like to sleep where they potty, and making it harder to potty at one end of the crate and lie down at the other end will make housetraining easier. While you're housetraining, or if your pup is prone to ripping things to shreds, you may want to forego bedding of any kind in his crate.

Your pup's crate can be used for a time-out if he needs one (tired puppies often do), but don't use the crate for punishment. Your dog should think of his crate as a good, safe place. Rather than shoving him forcibly into his crate, toss a toy or treat in and say, "Crate" or "Kennel." Praise him when he gets in, and quietly close the door. Feed him his meals in his crate, at least for a while, and if possible, have your pup sleep in his crate in your bedroom at night.

How long should a dog be crated at one time? The general rule for a puppy is his age in months plus one. So if your puppy is two months old, don't crate him for more than three hours at a stretch. If he's six months old, don't crate him any longer than seven hours. Older dogs can usually last at least seven or eight hours. These are, of course, rough guidelines, as individuals vary. If your three-month-old puppy seems to tolerate four hours between breaks but wets his crate if you leave him for half an hour longer, then don't expect him to hold it longer than four hours for now.

Many people have to work all day, but if you have to be gone all day, please make plans for your Boxer's comfort before he joins your household. It's particularly unfair to ask a puppy to spend eight or nine hours alone, and worse to ask him not to potty for that long. You might consider hiring a reliable pet sitter or dog walker to come in during the day if you can't come home to let your pup out for a little while.

Give your puppy something to occupy himself while he's crated—a safe chew toy will give him something to do. Don't leave him with anything he can rip apart and swallow.

Housetraining

Most dog owners consider housetraining to be the first and most important kind of training a puppy needs. If you're careful to take your puppy out when he needs to potty and patient when he has the occasional accident, housetraining your Boxer should go quickly and smoothly. If you've adopted an adult Boxer who hasn't been housetrained, the guidelines that follow apply as well, with the added advantage that, assuming he's healthy, your dog will have better control of his bodily functions.

The first principle of housetraining is patience. Your puppy is a baby and doesn't have complete control of his bladder or bowels. By the time he knows he has to go, he may not be able to hold it any longer. It's your job—not his—to keep your puppy off the Persian carpet until he's reliable and to teach him where he should potty.

Most puppies signal when they're going to potty, so when your pup is loose in the house, watch him closely. If he begins turning in circles, sniffing the floor, or arching his back while walking, pick him up and take him out. Don't expect him to walk out the door once he starts to potty.

A crate is an essential training tool.

Take your pup out to potty after every meal, first thing in the morning, last thing at night, whenever he wakes up, after active play, and when you hear him stirring in the middle of the night. Take him on leash to the place you want him to use. Don't play with him until he's finished. If he doesn't go within 10 minutes, crate him for 10 to 15 minutes, and then take him out again. When he potties, reward him with praise and a treat or short playtime. Wait a few minutes before you take him in—puppies don't always do everything right away, so give him time to be sure he won't go again in three minutes.

If your pup does soil the floor because no one was watching him, you need to remove all trace of odor from that spot. Regular cleaners aren't enough; remember, your Boxer has a much better nose than you do. If he smells traces of urine or feces, he'll think he's found the toilet. Pet supply stores carry special cleansers designed to eliminate odors. For urine odors (but not feces) you can also use an inexpensive 50-50 mixture of white vinegar and water.

Never yell at your puppy or punish him for accidents, and definitely do not rub his nose in it. Such methods are not only abusive, they're ineffective. If you must scold someone, scold yourself for giving your pup the chance to make a mistake. Your Boxer won't pee in the house to annoy you or get even. He'll do it because he has to go and hasn't yet learned to tell you to open the door. And don't scold him—you can rant until your tongue falls out, but your pup still won't understand why you're upset about urine on the new carpet. Just clean up, and supervise your pup more closely.

Here are a few other tips for successful housetraining:

- If you buy a puppy, buy from a responsible breeder who has kept her puppies in clean surroundings and perhaps already started housetraining. Puppies who spend their first weeks in filth are notoriously difficult to housetrain.
- Feed your pup high-quality dry food. His stools will be smaller and more compact, and he'll be better able to control his bowels.
- Don't give your puppy or dog the run of the house until he's reliably housetrained. Keep him in the room you're in, and watch him closely.
- Feed your pup at the same time every day, and try to get up and go to bed on a regular schedule until he's reliably housetrained.
- While you're housetraining your pup, feed him at least four hours before bedtime, and don't let him drink water within two hours of bedtime.
- Keep your puppy's potty place clean and free of feces. He doesn't want to step in it any more than you do.

It can take several months to housetrain a puppy to be fully reliable, partly because your pup won't have complete physical control of his bladder and bowels until he's an adult. But if your Boxer is still having frequent accidents in the house at six months or older, talk to your veterinarian to rule out medical problems. If you don't have the time or patience to housetrain a puppy, an older puppy or adult who is already trained is a better choice for you.

Leash Training

Polite leash skills are essential for your big, strong Boxer. You should be able to go for a walk without your dog pulling you down the street or wrapping the leash around your legs, and you should be able to control him safely on a leash when necessary.

First, be sure your dog is wearing an appropriate collar that fits him properly and that your leash is long enough to allow him reasonable freedom of movement but not so long that it's hard for you to manage. If you're training a puppy, or if your Boxer is responsive and submissive to you, try the "no forward progress" response to pulling first: If your pup pulls, stop and stand still until he stops pulling. It may take him awhile to notice that you're not moving, but when he does, praise him and continue walking. If he pulls again, halt. Your walks may be short for a few days, but your dog will soon figure out that pulling is counter-productive, while polite walking keeps him moving.

Some dogs, though, are much too determined about their own pursuits to respond to this passive approach. If stopping in place doesn't work, change directions so that pulling not only keeps your dog from moving toward the object of his desire, but it actually results in moving him away from it. To do this, grasp your leash and set your hands together in front of your waist so that you don't jerk your dog with your hands. When he starts to pull, turn and walk in a different direction. Don't wait for him, and don't talk to him until he catches up with you.

When he does, praise him, and try turning back in the original direction. Give him a treat occasionally. Most dogs quickly learn to pay attention and not to pull.

Some puppies and dogs are just so determined to see what's up ahead that they need more control. If your Boxer simply isn't responding, you may need to try an obedience class (or another one if you've been through one already).

Because Boxers can be strong pullers, it is important to teach them how to walk nicely on leash.

FIVE ESSENTIAL COMMANDS

Come, sit, down, stay, and leave it—these five basic commands are essential, and even puppies can learn them. There are many ways to teach each of these behaviors, of course. I'll tell you how I teach them so you can get started training your Boxer. You should still take your dog through at least one obedience class, and I would suggest you read a variety of training books and articles as well. No single method works for every dog or person, so if one isn't working for you, look for an alternative.

Come

A reliable response to the come command is one of the most important things you can teach your Boxer. Most

Doggy School

Most of your dog's training is, of course, done at home or out and about. But to be effective as a trainer, you need to learn how to communicate well with your dog. Good training books and articles will certainly help, but nothing can replace the benefits of a good obedience class taught by a qualified instructor who shows you how to train your dog. A good class also gives your pup a chance to socialize with people and other dogs and gives you a supportive environment in which to learn and work with your dog, surrounded by other people who also love dogs.

If you have a young puppy, a good puppy kindergarten class will help you get his training started and promote good social skills. Puppy kindergarten classes usually meet once a week for four to eight weeks, and naturally you'll have homework. Puppies can learn basic commands such as sit, down, come, and stay for short periods, as well as skills that will be used in more advanced training later, but don't expect your puppy to perform perfectly. For an older puppy or dog, or a pup who has successfully completed puppy kindergarten, a basic obedience class is your best bet. Look for one that teaches manners and promotes social skills.

If you plan to participate eventually in canine sports, look for an instructor who understands your goals. Early training should provide a foundation for later advanced training, and ideally your instructor will help you and your dog avoid developing habits that you will later have to unlearn. Young dogs shouldn't perform strenuous activities, like jumping and weaving through poles, until their bones and joints mature. However, they can still learn to pay attention and follow directions. Beware of anyone who promises you a fully trained dog in a few weeks. If the results offered seem too good to be true, they are. Although some dogs and people are quicker than others to learn certain skills, no dog or dog owner is fully trained in six or eight weeks. Obedience training should be aimed at creating a dog-owner partnership built on two-way communication and respect without resorting to intimidation or abuse, so look for an instructor who uses positive, motivational training methods.

people want their dogs to come when called for the sake of convenience, and that can certainly be important—nobody wants to chase a disobedient dog around the backyard in the rain! More critically, a dog who comes reliably is safer than one who doesn't.

Begin with your puppy or dog on a leash or in a *very* small room or fenced area so that he can't go very far. Have a toy he likes or a small, yummy treat. Say, "Spot, come!" only one time in a happy, playful voice. Do whatever you have to do other than repeating the command to get your dog to come to you. Act silly, walk or run the other way, crouch down, or play with the toy. If he absolutely won't come on his own, gently pull him in with the leash. If he starts to come on his own after you pull, great—stop pulling. If not, gently reel him in. When he gets to you, on his own or with a little help, praise and reward him. Then let him return to whatever he was doing before you called. Repeat the process two or three times, then quit. Do this several times a day if possible.

If you're not the only human in the household, you can make a group game of teaching your dog to come. Call him back and forth or from one person to another. Just make sure that only one person calls at a time and that each person rewards the dog for coming.

Sounds simple, you think, but in reality most of the pet dogs you know don't come when their people call, do they? That's because too many people teach their dogs to ignore them. Let's see how you can make sure you don't inadvertently teach your Boxer to blow off the come command. (These principles apply to other training, too.)

• Always make obeying your command a safe and wonderful thing to do. When you call your dog, he should believe that you are the safest, most fun place he could be, and it's up to you to teach him this. Never call your dog to you for something he finds unpleasant, and never punish him for anything after calling him to you.

- Always praise your dog for coming when you call, and from time to time reward him as well with a treat, toy, or belly rub—something he likes.
- Always use the same word when you call. Common commands to call a dog include "come" or "here," although the exact word doesn't matter. Just don't confuse your dog by being inconsistent with the word you choose.
- Never repeat the command—that simply teaches your dog to ignore you. If he doesn't come when you call, go get him and put his leash on. Then, call him once and pull him in with the leash. Don't forget to praise and reward him for coming!
- Never let your dog off leash in an unfenced area if he doesn't come reliably—this means that he comes on the first command every single time he's called, even if there are squirrels or other distractions in the area. That level of reliability is not common! Even if your dog is fairly reliable, be extremely cautious. Leashes save lives.
- Never give a command you can't enforce, especially while you're teaching the command. If you can't trust your dog to come when you call, put him on a leash or long line when he goes out to potty in the cold, wet, dark yard. If he learns that he must always obey, eventually he won't think of not obeying—most of the time, at least!

Sit

Sit can be used to gain control of your dog and give him something to do instead of something you don't want him to do, like jumping on you or spinning in circles while you try to put his leash on. Most dogs seem to learn to sit on cue in certain situations even if they never learn any other command, because people often reward sits with food—or perhaps the dogs train us to do that! Sitting can be handy at other times, too, so it's a good command to teach even when you aren't offering dinner or treats. If you plan to compete in obedience or agility, a good sit response is essential.

The sit command can be used to gain control of your Boxer if he's engaged in an undesirable behavior.

Start with your dog on leash or confined in a small space. Hold a small treat in front of his nose, but don't let him take it. Close your fist over it if necessary. When your dog shows interest, *slowly* raise the treat just high enough to clear his head and move it slowly toward his tail. As his head comes up to follow the treat, his butt has to go down (unless you lift the treat too high, in which case he'll probably jump for it). When your dog starts to bend his hind legs to sit, say, "Sit" as you continue to move the treat slowly backward. The instant his fanny hits the floor, praise and reward him with the treat, then release him. If he stands up before you release him, don't give the treat—you'll be rewarding him for getting up, not for sitting. Just have him sit again, and give him the treat before you release him. Repeat three or four times, then quit.

When your dog sits promptly on command, start requiring him to sit for a longer time before you give him the treat, and have him continue to sit after the treat before you release him. Eventually you can wean away the treat, rewarding him with praise for sitting and with play and praise for the release. Your dog should eventually sit on the first command and stay sitting without another command until you release him.

Down

Teach your dog to lie down on command no matter where he is or what he's doing. Most people teach their dogs to down from a sit, but I like to teach the down from a stand for three reasons. First, a quick response to the down can save his life. Suppose your Boxer gets loose and is across a street. A car is coming. Obviously you don't want him to come to you, but you do want some control. I've also found that frightened or confused dogs are more likely to respond to the down than to come.

My other two reasons are less dramatic. Efficiency is one—getting your dog to sit and then lie down requires two

Your Boxer should learn to heed the down command no matter where he is or what he's doing.

commands. Not a big deal usually, but I prefer to get to the behavior I want with a single command whenever possible. Finally, if you plan to compete in obedience beyond the Novice level, your dog will have to perform a "moving down" in Open and a "signal down" in Utility. It's much easier to teach your dog those maneuvers if he doesn't think he has to sit in order to lie down. If he's already trained to lie down from a sit, that's fine. If you want to teach him to do it from a stand, consider using a different command—I've heard people use "drop," "crash," and other words.

Start with your dog standing. You may want to kneel at first rather than bending over each time. Hold a treat in your hand and slowly move your hand under your dog's chin toward his front legs, lowering it as you go. As his head follows the treat, he should fold himself into a down position. If his fanny stays up, gently guide it down. As soon as he's all the way down, praise him and give him the treat. When he's responding to the moving treat by folding quickly backward into a down, add your command, telling him, "Down" (or your other word) as you begin. When he's doing that quickly and reliably, give him the command, but don't move your hand toward him. When he's down, praise and reward. Be sure to give him the treat while he's down, not after he jumps up! Slowly increase the length of time he has to stay down before getting the treat—you don't want him to learn to be a jack-in-the-box. When he's reliable with you standing close to him, start giving the command when he's farther away (add distance very slowly) or moving.

If your pup steps back instead of lying down, move your hand with the treat toward him and down a little faster. You can use very light pressure between his shoulder blades to guide him into the down if necessary. If his butt stays up when his front end is down, press lightly on his hips. If he doesn't go down, don't try to force him. Keep the treat close to the ground with one hand, and cradle his hind legs from behind with the other, gently moving your arm forward around the hind legs until he folds down. Then praise and reward him.

Stay

"Stay" tells your dog not to move from whatever position he's in until you release him. I teach the stay initially in the down position because it's the easiest for the dog to hold without moving. If he learns the concept of staying while he is in a down, he'll learn to stay in a sit and a stand more easily.

Have your dog lie down. When he is completely down, tell him, "Stay." If he starts to get up, put him back in the down position. Don't repeat the command—he needs to learn to remember it and respond on the first command. When he has stayed down a few seconds, praise, reward, and release him, in that order. Start with very short stays—less than a minute—and stand close to your dog. Very slowly, increase the time until he will stay five minutes with you standing close to him.

When your dog is reliable for five minutes with you right there, tell him, "Down" and "Stay," and take one step away from him. Have him stay for 30 seconds, then step back, praise, reward, and release. Build the time up slowly to five minutes. Repeat this process as you increase distance, reducing the length of time and building it back up every time you add distance. If your dog starts popping up, fidgeting, or whining before the time is up, stand a little closer for a few days until he's comfortable again with that distance for that length of time. Then proceed to add distance.

Don't forget that you must release your dog before he's allowed to move out of a stay. Don't let him decide for himself when he's finished. Use the stay command only when you will be present to release your dog, not to keep him from running out the door when you're leaving for an evening out!

Practice down-stays in different environments. It's important that your Boxer learn to stay just as reliably away from home as in the comfort of your living room. Of course, make sure you're always in a position to restrain him if necessary—if you practice in a squirrel-infested park, keep him on a leash or long line! Practice stays while you're doing other things around the house. Just don't forget that you told him to stay; don't let him wander away, and don't forget to come back and release him. If you want your dog to obey commands reliably, you have to give them reliably, too.

When your dog understands and obeys the stay command when he's lying down, repeat the same process to teach him to sit and stay. Don't cut corners on time and distance; to your dog, a sit-stay and a down-stay are completely different. Be patient, and keep time and distance

Teach your dog to let you take things from him, not to fight you for possession of resources.

short until your dog is really dependable. Establishing a solid foundation at this stage of training will save you a lot of frustration and remedial training later.

Leave It!

"Leave it" tells your dog that he's not allowed to touch or chase something that has piqued his interest. It's a useful command in many situations and has saved many a ham sandwich from pilfering canine jaws!

To teach "leave it" successfully, you need to make sure that your dog knows two things: Obeying you is more rewarding than obtaining the object of his desire, and in any case he'll never get the thing he's after. To convey these points, you must reward your dog for leaving whatever he covets with something he considers worthwhile. You must also control the situation so that your dog cannot get whatever he's after. If he does, his disobedience is self-rewarding. So, as when teaching him to come when called, if you can't enforce the leave it command when you're teaching it, don't use it.

A caution before you begin: If your Boxer has a tendency to guard food or other resources, don't try to teach the leave it command on your own. Get professional help from an experienced trainer or a qualified behaviorist. And regardless of your dog's behavioral history, teach children never to take things from a dog, even a dog they know. If the dog has something he shouldn't, teach the kids to tell an adult.

To teach "leave it," your dog must be on leash—if you can't control the situation, he'll only learn to ignore you. Start by putting something that you know your dog will find interesting on or near the floor. Don't use his regular toys or food, because that would not be fair. Use something he's never seen before or that he's not allowed to have but will probably try to pick up or investigate. Have some wonderful treats ready—maybe something extra special like tiny bits of cheese or meat. Put your dog on his leash, walk him near the target object, and be sure the leash is short so you can prevent him from getting it. As soon as he shows interest in the object, say, "Leave it!" and walk quickly away. He'll have to follow you because of the leash. (You can also pull the dog away, but I like to keep moving so the dog refocuses quickly.) As soon as your dog looks at you instead of the object, praise him and give him a treat. Make a big fuss about what a good dog he is. Repeat the process three or four times, then quit. Be sure to remove the object before you remove your dog's leash. If you do this a few times a day, your dog should learn "leave it" quickly, but be aware of potential training hazards.

If your dog gets the target object, take it away from him if you can do so safely. Do not try to take anything from your dog if he growls or guards it! You could get bitten. Again, get professional help to stop such behavior at the first sign.

Once your Boxer learns to leave things alone when you tell him, you won't need to reward him with treats, but do always praise lavishly for obeying this command, and do something fun to make up for his disappointment. We all know how hard it is to resist temptation!

PROBLEM BEHAVIORS

With careful planning and quick responses, you can prevent most problem behaviors and eliminate most others fairly easily. First, you need to figure out why your dog is doing what he's

Keeping your Boxer mentally and physically stimulated can help prevent problem behaviors.

doing. Is he acting on an instinct? Is he bored and full of energy? Have you inadvertently taught him an obnoxious behavior that gets the results he wants? Is your Boxer training you instead of the other way around? If he barks at you, do you hop up and hand him a biscuit? If so, you're not alone—lots of smart dogs train their owners. You can redirect the situation by either completely ignoring him (a behavior that is never rewarded disappears) or by requiring him to do something to earn what he wants.

It's easier to teach your dog to do *something* than to teach him to do *nothing*. If he does something you don't like, give him an acceptable alternative. If he takes your slipper, take it from him and give him a dog toy.

Prevention works wonders, too. If your Boxer can't be trusted, crate him when you can't watch him. If your dog digs holes when he's alone in the yard for 20 minutes, don't leave him alone in the yard for more than 15 minutes. If he hasn't learned to come when you call him, don't let him off leash.

Also, be sure your Boxer gets plenty of exercise. Remember, his ancestors were developed to have the

Give your pup plenty of toys but not all at once. If all of his toys are available all the time, they'll lose their appeal. Give your dog two or three toys at a time—something hard to chew on, something he can roll and chase, and something soft that he can shake and "kill." Switch the toys with others every day or two.

stamina to work long hours, so he has lots of energy that needs to be channeled into safe exercise, and you need to help him. Very few dogs self-exercise, and if yours does, he'll very likely do things you won't like in the process.

Your Boxer's mind also needs exercise. Some dog toys are designed to provide mental stimulation—hard plastic cubes that randomly dispense bits of food as the dog rolls them interest some dogs. Advanced training relieves boredom and the behavior problems it causes, provides physical exercise, and makes for a better companion. Even if you don't work on preventing or solving a specific problem, training your dog makes him more secure and builds his trust in you, and that usually results in better behavior across the board. Obedience, agility, tricks, tracking, and other sports are all open to Boxers, and you don't have to compete to reap their benefits.

Digging

Many dogs like to dig. If your Boxer smells or hears evidence of little furry animals under the surface of the ground, he'll want to unearth them. If he has a bone or other treasure, he might decide to bury it. If you leave your Boxer alone in the yard, he might try his paw at landscaping to relieve his boredom and expend his energy.

A determined digger can quickly turn a lovely yard into a moonscape, and you almost certainly will want to keep that from happening where you live. You could supervise all of your dog's outdoor time, but that's not a practical solution for most people. Fortunately, you can discourage and redirect inappropriate digging. Some of these methods work with some dogs (not all), but if you're at least as smart and determined as your Boxer, you can have your dog and a normal yard as well.

Solution

Not all Boxers are serious diggers, but if yours is, why not give him his own personal recreational digging spot? Pick a place with loose sand or sandy soil, which is cleaner than clay or loam and a lot more fun to send flying. Build your dog a sandbox if necessary, making sure the sand is deep enough that he can really dig in and that you have a barrier to control the flying sand or dirt. Bury a toy or treat, bring your pup to the spot, and let him sniff. Encourage him to dig and praise him when he does. Then, encourage him to find the buried treasure. Repeat the process over a few days. In the meantime, if you see your dog digging in a different part of the yard, say, "Leave it" and take him to his permitted digging spot. Don't leave him alone in the yard until you're confident that he won't dig in the wrong places.

Ensuring that your Boxer gets lots of physical and mental exercise will also help prevent unwanted digging by giving him other outlets for his energy. Even practicing basic obedience skills, playing retrieving games, and learning a few tricks help, and more advanced training in obedience, agility, tracking, and other sports is even better.

If your Boxer tends to dig in one particular illegal spot, try filling or covering his hole with rocks, a pot, or some other dig-proof barrier. You can also bury chicken wire under the top layer of soil in a garden—plants will still be able to grow, but your dog's digging will be curtailed. Fencing or wire buried horizontally or vertically also helps keep dogs from tunneling under fences.

Be sure that you don't inadvertently encourage your Boxer to dig. Bonemeal and bloodmeal used as soil additives in a garden, for example, will entice your dog with the promise of buried prey, so think before you bury or spread anything in your yard.

A variety of substances are touted as useful for deflecting diggers, but many of them are only marginally effective, and some are dangerous. Commercial products are available that are supposed to stop digging, but they don't always work. Black and cayenne pepper sprinkled on top of the soil stop some dogs, but others don't seem to notice. Mothballs have been used for many years to repel animals, but they are highly toxic. The biggest drawback of using products to repel your dog is that while you may halt his digging in some areas, you don't provide him with an alternative behavior. He still has the energy and drive that made him dig in the first place. You can be sure that he'll find another outlet, and you may not like what he comes up with any better than you liked his digging. The best solution to digging is to redirect his energy and instinct into something you and he can both live with.

Chewing

Gnawing on a raw knuckle bone or a safe, hard chew toy is the canine equivalent of a good book or computer game.

If your Boxer enjoys gnawing on your favorite things, try replacing them with a safe chew toy.

It relieves stress, dispels boredom, eases the discomfort of teething, and is just plain enjoyable. Chewing only becomes a problem when your Boxer gnaws on the wrong things. You'll have to help him figure out what he's allowed to chew, because if your dog chews the wrong things, he can wreck your possessions and hurt himself.

Puppies and adolescent dogs are especially prone to chewing. Your puppy's deciduous (baby) teeth begin to come in when he is about four weeks old. When he's four to five months old, his deciduous teeth loosen, fall out, and are replaced by permanent (adult) teeth. During this process, his gums become swollen and sore, and he'll chew whatever he can grab to relieve his discomfort. Some dogs continue to enjoy chewing throughout their lives; others rarely chew as adults.

Solution

As with other problem behaviors, prevention is the ideal treatment. Begin by putting anything you don't want him to grab out of his reach. Don't underestimate a determined Boxer! Locked away out of sight is much safer than simply up high—Boxers have been known to scale amazing heights to snatch things from shelves and other elevated areas.

After you have done this, teach your dog that he may chew some things but not everything. If he picks up something he shouldn't, take it from him gently and give him one of his toys. Don't yell or punish him. That won't teach him what's right, and it may lead to other unwanted behaviors. Be smart, too—don't give him old shoes or socks to play with and then pretend you're surprised when he chews your good ones! Be consistent and think ahead, and your Boxer will soon learn what he's allowed to do.

If your Boxer is prone to chewing and ripping things, then he should *never* be left unsupervised where he can get to things he shouldn't have. This is a simple and sensible solution, and it's much kinder than letting your dog chew something that injures him. Confine your Boxer to his crate with a nice chew toy or a large, raw natural knucklebone to play with when you can't watch him.

Barking

Barking is a natural means of communication for a dog. Your dog might bark a greeting, a warning, or an invitation

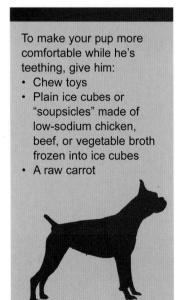

To make your pup more comfortable while he's teething, give him:
- Chew toys
- Plain ice cubes or "soupsicles" made of low-sodium chicken, beef, or vegetable broth frozen into ice cubes
- A raw carrot

to play, and some dogs bark just for fun. In the setting of your home, your dog will quickly learn that he can often get something he wants by barking. He probably barks to go out, to come in, to initiate play, and to get your attention, and chances are you understand him and respond. He may also bark to alert you to happenings around your home—a stranger at the door, a dog passing on the sidewalk, or a chipmunk on the front porch.

Barking is difficult to stop because it's self rewarding for your dog, and most people find a reasonable amount of canine vocal activity acceptable and even comforting at times. But if your dog barks too often or won't stop once he starts, you (and your neighbors) will probably find it anything but comforting. The good news is that problem barking—that is, barking that exceeds reasonable levels—can usually be controlled if you're willing to invest some time and effort. In the meantime, be considerate of other people; nothing is more annoying than a constantly barking neighborhood dog. Let your neighbors know that you're trying to solve the problem. Even if they haven't complained to you (or the police) about the racket, you can be sure they've noticed it.

Don't leave your dog outdoors when you're not home. It's not a great idea anyway, but it is particularly inappropriate if you own a barker.

Solution

If your dog barks excessively, try to figure out why. Is he bored? Does he spend a lot of time alone or get insufficient exercise? Do sights and sounds around your home and yard excite him and stimulate his barking? Finding the reason behind excessive barking often leads to a fairly simple solution.

Simply increasing your dog's daily exercise may help curb his barking if he does it out of boredom. Go back to regular training activities. Even if your dog doesn't bark in class and it doesn't seem that you're addressing the problem, training often has a ripple effect on a dog's behavior. Besides, the time you spend with your dog in class and doing your homework is time he spends using his brain in directed activity rather than yapping about how bored he is.

Dogs also bark to sound an alert when they perceive an "intruder." If the threat happens to be a burglar, barking is good. If it's your neighbor taking the garbage out or working in her garden, you probably want your dog to stop barking when you tell him to. Again, obedience training will help by giving you a way to direct your dog to alternative behaviors. When he starts to bark at someone, have him sit or lie down and stay. Put his leash on if necessary so that he has to pay attention to you. When he's quiet, praise and reward him.

It may help also to introduce your dog to neighbors he's bound to see around "his" territory. Teach him that having people around is a good thing. Have a neighbor or a friend walk by your yard. If your dog remains quiet, tell him how good he is and give him a treat. If he barks, tell him, "Down" or "Stay" and praise and reward him as soon as he's quiet. Repeat the process several times a day for several days, having the "intruder" come closer as your dog becomes quieter and steadier on the stay. Try to enlist the help of different people (maybe some friends from obedience class) so that he can generalize the quiet principle to whoever walks by. If your dog is indoors watching from the window, you can use the same method; have him lie down and be quiet, and praise and reward him. Consistency is essential for success. Don't ignore your dog's barking one time, encourage it the next, and yell at him the time after that. Although it's unlikely you'll ever completely stop your Boxer from barking, he should become more tolerant and controllable.

Barking can also be part of other behavioral issues that need to be addressed before the barking will subside. Dogs with separation anxiety often bark excessively. Dogs who are highly territorial or who are fearful due to lack of proper socialization often bark at anyone or anything. And don't believe the old adage that barking dogs don't bite—the only dog who has ever given me a serious bite barked like crazy, lunged, bit, and went right back to barking.

Some people prefer to use modern electronics for a hopefully quick fix rather than investing time and effort in training. Bark collars are sold in discount stores as well as pet supply stores, and they promise a quick end to your dog's behavioral problems. The collars are supposed to discourage barking by administering an automatic punishment—an electrical shock, spray of citronella aimed at the dog's nose, or a high-pitched sound. Although bark collars seem to offer a simple solution, they treat the symptoms rather than the cause. If your dog barks to relieve his boredom, he'll very likely replace the racket with a different but equally undesirable activity. If he barks out of fear or anxiety, a bark collar will probably increase his stress level, leading to more neurotic behaviors. If he's territorial or aggressive, he may hold the person or animal he sees as a threat responsible for his discomfort, and he may become aggressive toward that person or animal. Bark collars do work on some dogs but not all. I've heard many a dog bark while sporting a fully operational bark collar. Prevention, control, and training are the best ways to turn down the volume.

Jumping Up

If you're like most dog owners, you don't want your dog to jump up and plant muddy paw prints on your pants or rip your pantyhose with his nails. And truthfully, ruining your clothes is not his goal in jumping up. So why *does* your Boxer jump up? Well, he probably jumps up mostly because he likes you and he wants your attention. Besides, you and other people probably reward him for the behavior, at least sometimes, by petting him or getting excited and pushing him away, which he sees as play. When he's a baby, jumping up may be endearing, but an adolescent or adult Boxer who jumps on people is not only annoying, he's dangerous.

Some dogs may jump up because they have been encouraged to do so from the time they were puppies.

Solution

To teach your dog not to jump on you, you have to be consistent in your response when he does jump up, and you need to try to enlist the cooperation of other people who interact with your dog. If you have a puppy, teach him from the day you bring him home that jumping up doesn't get the results he wants. If you adopt an older Boxer who has not been taught that jumping up is unacceptable, the lesson may take a little longer to sink in because he has an old habit to break, but he can learn nevertheless.

One method that works if you do it right is to completely ignore your dog when he's jumping up. Fold your arms over your chest, turn your back on the dog, look up or away, and don't say a word. If you've been pushing him down before starting this method, your dog will keep trying for awhile,

but sooner or later he'll realize that jumping gets him a very boring human rather than an excited, active playmate, and he'll quit. When he does quit, calmly talk to him and pet him. If he jumps up again, go into boring mode. Once your dog knows that jumping on you gets him the opposite of what he wants, he'll stop doing it.

If you plan to use this approach, be patient and plan ahead. Don't go near your pup wearing anything except puppy-safe clothes until he's reliable about not jumping on you. You may have to plan ahead and invest a little time to accomplish this, but a few weeks of consistent training will pay off in years of living with a dog who doesn't jump on you. So if necessary, get up a little earlier, take care of your pup, and then confine him before you get dressed for work. When you get home, change your clothes before you let your dog out.

It's also important to be absolutely consistent. If you ignore your bouncing dog part of the time but reward him at other times by talking (loudly, no doubt), pushing him off, and getting excited, he'll continue to jump up in hopes of initiating a good game of "jump and play."

An alternative way to teach your dog not to jump up requires that you give him some additional obedience training (which he needs in any case). When you think he's about to jump on you or someone else, direct your dog to perform a different behavior—employing the sit or down commands will work well. When he performs as directed, praise him. Give him a treat or other reward while he's learning, and when he's reliable, simply praise him for a correct response.

Although many people use the alternative command method successfully, it has two big potential pitfalls. First, your dog needs to understand the command you give, and if he doesn't yet understand it, you have to teach him as you go. This is fine, but yelling, "Sit! Sit! Sit!" at an ever higher and more frantic volume as your dog leaps up won't teach him anything except that you are excitable. And that's the second problem with the method. Your smart little Boxer may learn that he can get you excited by jumping.

No matter how you teach your Boxer not to jump up, there are a few things you should *not* do. Don't put your hands on your dog to push him away or down, and don't follow the pushing down with petting. Attention is what he wants, and being pushed or petted rewards him for jumping. Wait until he gets off on his own, and then pet him. Don't knee, kick, or hit your dog for jumping up, either. Unless you're very coordinated, you probably won't connect, but if you do you could seriously injure your dog. You will also teach him not to trust you, and you could provoke a defensive response. It's much more effective and fair to teach your dog that calm, polite behavior gets him what he wants, and jumping up does not.

Anxiety or Fear

Separation anxiety is a condition in which a dog becomes worried and agitated in his owner's absence. Specific behaviors and combinations of behaviors vary, but the affected dog may bark, whine or howl, pace the floor, salivate or vomit, urinate or defecate, or become destructive.

Solution

Owners often create or contribute to separation anxiety by their own behavior when leaving and arriving home. If you act like being away from your dog is a horrible, frightening thing, your dog will pick up on your attitude and quite possibly follow suit. This is why it's important not to fuss over your dog when you leave or return home. Put your pup in his crate 10 to 15 minutes before you plan to leave so that he can relax. Give him a special treat that he gets only when you go out without him—a special chew toy or hollow bone stuffed with soft cheese or peanut butter and kibble, for example. Go about your business and ignore your dog once he's in his crate. If you have a puppy, you'll need to get him out to potty as soon as you come home, but if your dog is older and shows signs of separation anxiety, he can wait a little while. In that case, don't let him out immediately when you get home; let him calm down and get used to you being home.

If your Boxer is showing symptoms of separation anxiety, the first order of business is to protect your dog and your possessions when you're not home. If your dog isn't already crate trained, get a crate and teach him to be comfortable in it. Always crate him when you leave. Most dogs feel secure in their crates. If you give him a safe chew toy, he'll have a way to relieve his stress without hurting himself or anything else.

Basic obedience training will also help build your anxious dog's confidence. Teach him the stay command, and have him practice staying for different lengths of time while you go about your regular activities at home. Work up to stays of half an hour or longer, and teach him to stay even when you leave the room. Just don't forget to release him at some point! Having to stay in one place while you move around will help him understand that he doesn't have to be right beside you to be safe. Have him spend some time in his crate while you're home, too. That way he won't associate the crate strictly with your absence, and he'll know it's a safe haven whether you're at home or away.

Figure out how long after you leave that your dog becomes overly anxious, and then try leaving for periods shorter than that. If he starts to pace and whine when you've been gone five minutes, stay away for three minutes and then return. If he stayed relaxed—or at least didn't display overt anxiety—calmly praise him and reward him with a little treat or play session. If he was agitated, just ignore him until he relaxes. Don't pay any attention to him while he's still showing signs of anxiety—you don't want to reward him for being nervous. Try these short reconditioning sessions on weekends and in the evening. Even if you can't stay home for a month to help your dog conquer his fears, you can reduce his anxiety by teaching him that you won't always be gone for hours, and no matter how long you're gone, you will always come back and nothing bad will happen to him in the meantime.

Sometimes it also helps to place the crate in a particular part of the house. If your dog enjoys looking out the window, try placing his crate where he can see out. If that makes him more agitated, put his crate away from the windows so that he feels less vulnerable. Some dogs relax more if they hear voices or music, so try leaving a radio or television on with the volume down low. Your pup might also like to cling to something that smells like you—maybe an old sweatshirt that you haven't laundered since you last wore it. One of my dogs used to sleep with one of my shoes. If your Boxer is a chewer or ripper upper, of course, don't give him anything that can hurt him or vice versa.

If you have to be away from home for hours on end, it might be worth paying someone to come in during the day to let your dog out for awhile, especially if his anxiety hits him several hours after you leave. If your dog continues to be severely anxious when you're gone and your attempts to help him don't seem to be working, talk to your veterinarian or a qualified animal behaviorist. They may identify specific factors affecting your dog and your situation and be able to create an effective treatment plan in light of those factors. In extreme cases, antianxiety medication can be prescribed, but drugs are not a good long-term solution. Some people do report success with herbs, flower essences, and other unconventional treatments, and most won't hurt your dog, but there's no scientific evidence that proves their effectiveness.

Mouthing and Biting

Although Boxers tend to be fairly tolerant, they do have teeth that they can use in their own defense. This is why it's extremely important to lay down some rules of interaction from the very beginning. Rule number one, which your

puppy should begin to learn from your very first encounter, is that canine teeth do not belong on human skin, even in play. There's a good chance you'll need to teach this rule not only to your Boxer, but also to your human family, particularly the young males who love rough play.

But why are puppies so determined to mouth and nibble us? Think about how puppies and dogs play with their toys and with one another. They use their mouths! They bite, tug, grab, lick, and pull. Use of his mouth comes naturally to your puppy, and he'll probably mouth you until you teach him not to. He doesn't mean to hurt you, but puppy teeth are sharp and you aren't protected by fur like his mother and siblings.

In general, puppies mouth and nip humans because that is how they play with one another.

Solution

To protect yourself from damage during puppy play, and to instill the idea that he simply may not use his teeth on human beings, you need to teach your Boxer not to mouth and bite. I'll suggest two methods I've found effective.

First, make mouthing and biting counterproductive. The instant your pup puts his mouth on you, get up, walk away, and ignore him for a minute or so. Then, resume playing—

throw a toy, gently rub your pup's belly, or whatever you like as long as you don't encourage him to mouth you. Every time he does, get up and ignore him again. If he pulls on your clothes or bites your ankles, leave the room for a minute and ignore him. Then come back and resume play.

Another way to redirect your puppy's mouthy behavior is to give him something other than your hand to put in his mouth. If he mouths you when you're petting him or playing, gently offer him a toy and continue to pet him. He'll soon figure out that hands are good for belly rubs and ear scratches but are off limits for gnawing. If he insists on mouthing and biting you instead of the toy, use the method outlined earlier.

Many puppies get the idea very quickly, although some take a little longer. If ignoring your pup doesn't work after several tries, up the ante. Leave him completely alone for a minute or so, taking the toys with you if necessary. Then return and resume play. For this method to work, you need to encourage all members of your family to use it consistently, but if mouthing and nipping always drives your dog's playmates away, he'll soon quit.

Mouthing by those sharp puppy teeth is annoying and potentially painful, but it is normal puppy behavior. Aggression, on the other hand, manifested by serious growling, guarding, and biting, is something else entirely. A lot of puppy play sounds aggressive—puppies growl and snarl and bark at each other—but it is play. Think of it as a canine version of cops and robbers, with growls replacing "bang, bang!" The goal is to have fun and learn, not to cause serious injury. True aggression is not normal and is potentially dangerous to people and other pets. If your Boxer growls or bares his teeth at you or any other member of your family, snaps, or guards his food, toys, bed, or anything else from you, talk to his breeder, your veterinarian, or your obedience instructor. You might be misinterpreting normal Boxer puppy antics, but an occasional puppy or dog truly is unacceptably aggressive. Don't ignore aggression in the hopes that it will get better on its own. It won't. If your Boxer is aggressive or if you're not sure his behavior is normal, get help from a dog trainer or behaviorist who is qualified to deal with aggression or return the pup to the breeder. In the

meantime, don't take any chances, especially if you have children.

Never hit your Boxer for mouthing or nipping (or anything else, for that matter). Hitting doesn't train your dog and nearly always causes more problems than you had to start with. If your dog has the typical Boxer confidence and attitude, he may try to defend himself, putting you both in peril. Or he might think you're playing with him and respond by more excited nipping. If he's not so tough, he may become frightened and avoid you or bite out of fear. None of these reactions benefit you or your dog.

If mouthing and nipping are a problem with your dog, don't let anyone—especially children—play tug-of-war or other rough games that encourage him to compete with people for possession of things. Teach him to chase toys you throw and then give them to you to throw again.

No matter how reliable you believe your dog is, all interaction between him and children should be supervised by a responsible adult who can intervene immediately if necessary. If you're trying to teach your dog not to mouth or nip, the training should be done by an adult. Children tend to react to rough puppy play by screaming, jumping around, pushing the puppy away, and getting excited, which your pup will interpret as play. Kid and dog interactions can get out of control very quickly, and both participants can end up frightened or injured or both.

To keep your puppy from becoming cranky, make sure he gets enough rest after playtime.

Resource Guarding

Resource guarding is a common problem in dogs who are not taught that it's unacceptable. A resource is anything the dog perceives as having value, such as food, a toy, a dog bed, the couch, or even a person. Unchecked guarding behavior can escalate and become dangerous, but you can teach most dogs not to guard, particularly if you start when they're young.

Solution

Playing rough games that encourage your dog to challenge you for possession of things teaches him that it's acceptable to do so, the first step toward true resource guarding behavior. A more sensible thing to teach your dog from puppyhood on is that you control all that is good in his life—food, toys, access to play and exercise. Do this not through bullying but through basic obedience training and consistency. Have him perform an obedience command for you and then reward him.

It's not unusual for a dog, especially an adolescent, to try to climb the social ladder within his pack (canine and human), but if he does, it's essential that you reassert your authority. If your dog challenges you for control of anything—a toy, his food, your favorite chair—then he should lose his privileges. The toy should disappear (all toys if necessary). Dinner should come a few morsels at a time and only after he obeys a command. He should remain on the floor, off the furniture. Coupled with continuing work in basic obedience, most dogs accept their subordinate status quite easily. If guarding behavior is occurring between multiple dogs, you as the alpha should take possession of the object of their desire.

If your dog has already developed a pattern of aggressive resource guarding, get help from a qualified trainer or behaviorist.

Aggression

True aggression in dogs can be caused by a number of factors. Some dogs simply have bad temperaments, and some medical problems can contribute to aggressive behavior. Some dogs are aggressive toward people, others toward animals, and still others are aggressive toward anything that moves. An aggressive dog—one who threatens to bite, tries to bite, or does bite—is dangerous. Don't underestimate the ability of a dog to inflict damage if he means to.

Solution

If your dog acts aggressively, get qualified professional help immediately.

The first order of business should be a thorough physical examination, including a full thyroid panel (not just a thyroid screening). Be sure to tell your vet about the aggressive behavior. Hypothyroidism (low thyroid) can contribute to aggressive behavior, as can other medical conditions. Ask your vet whether other tests would be useful. If your Boxer isn't already neutered, have the surgery done. Altering reduces aggression in both males and females, especially if it's done before the dog reaches sexual maturity. When a physical cause for aggression can be identified, it may be possible to stop the behavior with treatment.

Training takes some time and effort, but it really is the kindest, most loving thing you can do for your Boxer. No one wants to live with an out-of-control canine brat, for one thing. For another, your Boxer is an intelligent animal, and he will thrive on learning new things. He will also respect and love you more for teaching him what you want and expect from him!

ADVANCED TRAINING AND ACTIVITIES
FOR YOUR BOXER

The Boxer is an extremely versatile dog, able to excel at a variety of sports and activities. If you find, as many people do, that you enjoy the time you spend training your dog and being with other "dog people," you might want to try some of the activities described in this chapter. Whether you participate in dog sports just for fun, to earn titles, or to strive for high-level awards and honors, the time you spend will help channel some of that Boxer enthusiasm into safe, nondestructive, and even productive activity. Most importantly, these activities will enhance the bond you share with your dog.

NONCOMPETITIVE ACTIVITIES FOR BOXERS

Most people own dogs purely for the pleasure of their company, with no practical or competitive motives whatsoever. And with the right person—someone who is active and assertive enough to channel the dog's energy and attitude into safe activities—the Boxer is an outstanding four-legged friend. Let's look at some of the activities you might pursue for the pure and simple pleasure of spending time with your dog.

Walking, Jogging, and Running

Walking, jogging, or running are great ways to keep you and your Boxer in shape, and if you use good sense and take a few precautions, they are safe and pleasurable activities for dog and human alike. Let's see how you can make the most of your outings on foot and paw.

Before you start any exercise program, be sure you and your dog are both in good health. If you haven't had checkups in a while, make appointments for both of you. Make sure your dog's nails are trimmed to a healthy length and that his footpads are in good condition. If your dog is overweight or out of condition, or if he's elderly or has been ill or injured, ask your vet about a diet and appropriate distance to walk, jog, or run in the beginning. Start slowly and build up.

Teach your Boxer to walk politely on leash before you take him for walks away from your own property or training class. Be sure, too, that whoever walks the dog can control the dog. If a child wants to walk your dog, the same rule applies; if the child can't control the dog under all circumstances, don't let her walk the dog without a responsible adult. Dog walkers should be capable of making quick decisions, too. Some walking hazards (encounters with stray dogs, for instance) are difficult even for adults to manage and can be downright dangerous for a child.

Always keep your dog on leash when you're in public. Leash laws make this mandatory in many places, but consideration for other people and animals and for your dog's safety make a leash vital as well. Be sure your dog's collar fits properly so that he can't slip out of it. Be sure the bolt on your leash is secure and that the leash is in good condition as well. Keep a firm grip on your leash. I *do not* recommend, though, that you slip your hand through the loop. A quick jerk by a squirrel-happy Boxer can break your wrist. I've seen it happen! Teach children, too, not to slide their hands through the loop, and never ever to put a leash around their neck or waist.

Please be considerate of your neighbors—pick up after your dog. You may not enjoy the job, but think how much more unappealing it is to clean up after someone else's dog. Disposable pooper-scoopers are available commercially, but plastic bags or disposable plastic gloves are cheaper and just as effective. Here's how to do it:
- Turn the bag inside out over your hand, or put the glove on.
- Pick up the poop with your "plastic hand."
- Pull the edge of the bag or glove down over your hand, capturing the poop, and pull your hand out.
- Tie a knot to seal the bag or glove.
- Dispose of the bag or glove in a proper receptacle (at home if necessary).

In very hot weather, keep outings short or go when it's cooler, early in the morning or in the evening. Concrete and blacktop get very hot in the sun. They can burn your dog's footpads and may reflect enough heat to cause heatstroke. Keep in mind that the short muzzle that is part of the Boxer's charm also makes him less able to cool himself in hot weather, so you need to be careful.

Try not to walk your dog where pesticides or herbicides have been used. If your dog does walk though a treated area, wash his feet with warm water and dog shampoo when you get home to prevent absorption or ingestion of toxic chemicals. If you like to walk or jog in the dark, put a reflective collar or vest on your dog, and wear light colors or reflective clothing yourself. Be cautious in very cold weather, too. Extremely low temperatures can cause hypothermia if your dog stays out too long. If salt or other chemicals have been used on the sidewalks and streets where you walk, wash your dog's feet with warm water after every walk. The chemicals and salt can irritate his feet, and they can be toxic if he licks them off.

Hiking and Backpacking

Boxers are natural companions for nature walks. They have the stamina for a hike, as well as the interest and senses to notice things we might overlook. If you hike with your Boxer, he'll make sure you stop to smell the roses. He'll also let you know when people and animals are nearby.

Your Boxer can learn to wear a backpack and carry his own food and water. (Build him up

Boxers enjoy participating in a variety of outdoor activities.

slowly to carrying weight.) He can also do his civic duty by carrying his feces out of the wilderness for proper disposal.

Whether you and your dog are going for an afternoon hike or a week-long adventure, you'll have more fun if you plan ahead. Be sure that dogs are permitted where you want to hike—they are not allowed in many national and state parks. If your dog is welcome, he must be under control at all times. Leashes are required by law in most places, and even if they're not, a leash will keep your Boxer safe, protect wildlife from his predatory urges, and keep him from disturbing your fellow hikers.

Some good basic equipment will make your outings safer and more pleasant. Your dog needs a collar that fits well and is in good condition, with his identification tag or tags, rabies tag, and license tag attached to it. Your leash will probably get dirty and wet, so you might prefer a nylon leash for hiking. If you use leather, which is easier on the hands than nylon, be sure to waterproof it and wipe it clean frequently. Retractable leashes are good in some situations, but they tend to wrap around trees and brush, and many parks require dogs to be on leashes 6 feet or shorter. Pack a spare collar and leash. They always seem to break 5 miles out

Naturally, your dog should be in good health when you take him hiking or backpacking, and his vaccinations should be up to date. Ask your veterinarian about vaccine recommendations—your dog could encounter bacterial and viral diseases in natural areas that he wouldn't around your neighborhood. He should also be treated with an effective tick repellant and killer and be protected against mosquito-borne heartworm disease.

into the journey. Carry water, and either bring a bowl for your dog or teach him to drink from a squirt bottle. You can find easy-to-carry collapsible bowls at pet supply stores. Offer your dog water at regular intervals to prevent dehydration and overheating. Don't let him drink from streams and other water sources along the way if you can help it; they are often contaminated with bacteria and chemicals. Finally, a few first-aid supplies may come in handy, too. Basics include tweezers in case your dog picks up a thorn or tick, antiseptic cleansing towels, and a topical antibiotic.

Remember that heatstroke is potentially fatal and that Boxers can overheat more quickly than longer-muzzled dogs. Hike in the early morning or evening and avoid the hottest parts of the day. If you will be at higher altitudes than your normal environment, allow extra time for breaks, and see that both you and your dog drink lots of water. Proper hydration helps fend off altitude sickness.

Good trail etiquette will go a long way toward making sure dogs remain welcome in parks and similar areas. Even a small dog can be intimidating to some people, so teach your buddy to sit or lie quietly beside the trail to let other hikers pass. Never hike with a dog you can't control or one who is a threat to people or other dogs.

The Canine Good Citizen® Test

The Canine Good Citizen (CGC) program was developed by the American Kennel Club to promote and reward well-behaved dogs as community members. To earn the CGC certificate, your dog must pass the Canine Good Citizen test, which consists of the following ten subtests:

1. *Accepting a friendly stranger*, who will approach and greet the dog's handler. The dog must remain quiet.
2. *Sitting politely for petting* while a friendly stranger pets the dog's head and body.
3. *Appearance and grooming* involves two steps. First, the evaluator checks that the dog is clean, groomed, and in good condition. Then, the dog must permit a stranger to comb or brush him and check his ears and front feet.
4. *Out for a walk* (walking on a loose lead) requires the dog to walk quietly on leash, making several turns and stops.
5. *Walking through a crowd* requires the dog and handler to walk politely among at least three people.
6. *Sit and down on command and staying in place* requires the dog to sit, lie down, and stay on command.
7. *Coming when called* requires the dog to stay on command, then come when called from a distance of 10 feet.
8. *Reaction to another dog* requires the dog to react with only casual interest when meeting another dog and handler.
9. *Reaction to distraction* requires the dog to react calmly to two common distractions (for instance, a chair falling over, a jogger running by, a wheeled cart passing by, or a dropped crutch or cane).
10. *Supervised separation* requires the dog to remain calm when left with the evaluator while his handler goes out of sight for three minutes.

The dog should wear a properly fitted buckle or slip (choke) collar made of leather, fabric, or chain during the test, and he needs to remain on leash for all subtests. When you arrive for the test, you must show written proof of rabies vaccination, and you should bring your dog's brush or comb for the grooming portion.

To earn the CGC, your dog must pass all ten sub-tests. If he growls, snaps, bites, or attacks or tries to attack a person or another dog, he'll be asked to leave. If you take the CGC test and don't pass the first time, don't give up! The test is a good way to see what you and your dog need to work on. Keep training, and try again later.

Animal Assisted Activities and Therapy

If you and your Boxer like people and enjoy volunteering, animal assisted activities (AAA) or animal assisted therapy (AAT) might be rewarding for you both.

The term "therapy dog" is often used as shorthand to refer to a dog who works with people in two different types of settings. As a participant in animal assisted activities (AAA), you and your dog will visit people in a variety of situations: nursing homes, literacy and reading programs,

The Kennel Club's Good Citizen Dog Scheme

In 1992, the Kennel Club launched a new training program called the Good Citizen Dog Scheme to promote responsible dog ownership in the UK. Since then, over 52,000 dogs have passed the test, which is administered through 1,050 training organizations.

Any dog is eligible to take part in the Good Citizen Dog Scheme, a noncompetitive plan that trains owners and dogs for everyday situations and grants four awards—bronze, silver, gold, and puppy foundation assessment—based on the level of training that both dog and owner have reached together.

For more information, refer to the Kennel Club's website at www.the-kennel-club.org.uk.

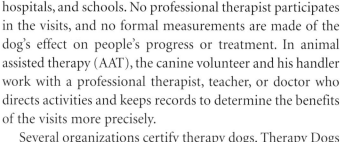

Therapy dogs are not the same as service dogs, who go through intensive training and then work as guide dogs for the blind, hearing dogs for the deaf, seizure alert dogs, general assistance dogs, and so on. Therapy dogs do not have the legal rights afforded to service dogs under the Americans with Disabilities Act.

hospitals, and schools. No professional therapist participates in the visits, and no formal measurements are made of the dog's effect on people's progress or treatment. In animal assisted therapy (AAT), the canine volunteer and his handler work with a professional therapist, teacher, or doctor who directs activities and keeps records to determine the benefits of the visits more precisely.

Several organizations certify therapy dogs. Therapy Dogs Incorporated (TDInc) certifies dog-and-handler teams that pass a basic test and several observations in a therapy setting. Therapy Dogs International, Inc., (TDI) uses a modified form of the AKC's Canine Good Citizen (CGC) test. The Delta Society offers several different types of certification and provides education for the handler. Some local organizations also offer certification.

You can make therapy visits to many places without being certified, but there are advantages to having your dog certified through a legitimate organization. Certification provides impartial assurance that your dog has the temperament and training needed to make him a good therapy dog, and it gives your dog and you more credibility. Most certifying organizations provide liability insurance to cover you and your dog while you're making official visits. The rules of the different organizations vary a bit, but all are meant to make therapy visits safe, comfortable, and pleasant for everyone involved.

Dog-and-handler teams sometimes work alone and sometimes with one or two other teams, which may include dogs, cats, or other animals. If you'd rather not make solitary visits, look for a local therapy group. Many obedience and kennel clubs have therapy groups, and some hospitals and nursing homes have their own programs. Some visiting situations may require your dog to sit or lie quietly while being petted, or he might be more active as he entertains people or "assists" a therapist. Whatever he does, he absolutely must like people and be reliable, and he must have some basic obedience training.

The rewards of therapy work are less tangible than ribbons and titles won in competition, but they are every bit as real. So is the potential for stress. Your dog will probably make it clear if he isn't enjoying the visits, but you need to be alert to subtle signs that he's unhappy in a particular

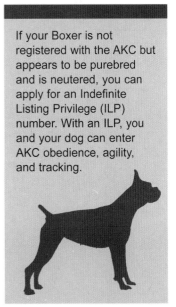

If your Boxer likes people and is reliably trained, he might make a good therapy or service dog.

environment. Some dogs like certain kinds of visits but not others. Your dog could also get burned out; he may just need a short break, or he may need to retire. Volunteer work and the cheer your dog brings to the people he visits are wonderful, but your own dog's welfare should always come first.

ADVANCED CANINE SPORTS

Many other people and dogs have discovered the fun of attending advanced classes together just for fun or to prepare for competition, so why not you? Whatever your reasons for continuing to train, working regularly with your Boxer will strengthen the bond between you and your dog and continue to direct some of that Boxer energy. Let's look at some of the activities you might choose to pursue.

Obedience

The sport of dog obedience demonstrates teamwork between the handler and dog. Boxers can and do succeed at obedience trials, but you need to remember that they are intelligent dogs who think for themselves. As a result, obedience training a Boxer can be challenging. The

If your Boxer is not registered with the AKC but appears to be purebred and is neutered, you can apply for an Indefinite Listing Privilege (ILP) number. With an ILP, you and your dog can enter AKC obedience, agility, and tracking.

successful trainer will find ways to engage the dog's interest and cooperation in learning and performing the obedience exercises. Like many intelligent dogs, Boxers are easily bored and will not perform the same exercise over and over. You will need to find ways to make the work fun and interesting for your dog. If you decide you want to earn obedience titles, you can participate in competitive programs offered by several organizations.

The American Kennel Club (AKC) obedience program is open to purebred dogs of breeds recognized by the AKC. It offers obedience titles at all levels, from Companion Dog (CD), Companion Dog Excellent (CDX), and Utility Dog (UD), to the UDX (Utility Dog Excellent) and OTCh (Obedience Trial Champion), and the ultra elite NOC (National Obedience Champion). To participate in AKC sports, your dog must be registered with the AKC.

The rules and requirements for titles vary from one competition program to another, but in general your dog must earn three legs, or qualifying scores, to earn a title. To earn a leg, he must score 50 percent on each exercise and have a total score of at least 170 out of 200 possible points. The skills required are progressively more difficult at each level.

Your dog may earn the Companion Dog (CD) title from the Novice class, which requires him to heel on and off leash at normal, slow, and fast speeds, wait where you tell him and come when called, stay on command in both a sit and a down with other dogs, and stand still while the judge touches him on the head and back. Novice A is for dogs who have not earned a CD and handlers who have never handled a dog to a CD. Novice B is for dogs who have not earned the CD shown by handlers who have handled other dogs to their CDs.

The Open class is for dogs who have earned the CD, and it leads to the Companion Dog Excellent (CDX) title. In Open, your dog must heel off leash and stay in a sit and a down with a group of dogs while you are out of his sight. He must drop to a down position on command while coming toward you, jump obstacles, and retrieve a dumbbell. Open A is for dogs who have not earned their CDXs. Open B is for dogs who have their CDXs but are continuing to compete.

Utility is for dogs who have earned the CDX, and it leads

The United Kennel Club (UKC) offers obedience titles for purebred and mixed-breed dogs. To participate, your dog must be registered with the UKC, but registration is simple with a Single Registration Application from the UKC. You can earn the U-CD, the U-CDX, and the U-UD. ("U" stands for "United.") If your dog excels at the sport, you can enter the annual "Top Gun" International Obedience Competition. For more information, visit the website at www.ukcdogs.com.

to the title of Utility Dog (UD). In utility, your dog must heel off leash, respond to hand signals, jump, and find articles by your scent. Utility A is for dogs who do not have their UDs. Utility B is for dogs who have their UDs but are continuing to compete.

Once your dog has earned the UD, he may continue to compete in Open B and Utility B. He will gain the title Utility Dog Excellent (UDX) by earning qualifying scores in both Open B and Utility B classes at ten shows. The title Obedience Trial Champion (OTCH) requires the dog to accumulate 100 points by earning placements in Open B and Utility B.

If you're competitive and willing to put in lots of hours of training, you can aim for high scores and advanced titles in obedience. If you aren't so competitive, you can still have a good time with your dog, earn your qualifying scores, and obtain your dog's titles. You'll also get to spend time with other people who love dogs, which most dog lovers consider a big plus.

When taking part in any outdoor activity, make sure to keep your Boxer cool—his short muzzle makes him prone to overheating.

KENNEL CLUB SPORTING EVENTS

The Kennel Club in the United Kingdom sponsors a variety of events for dogs and their owners to enjoy together. For complete listings, rules, and descriptions, please refer to the Kennel Club's website at www.the-kennel-club.org.uk.

Agility

Introduced in 1978 at Crufts, agility is a fun, fast-paced, and interactive sport. The event mainly consists of multiple obstacles on a timed course that a dog must handle. Different classes have varying levels of difficulty.

Flyball

Flyball is an exciting sport introduced at Crufts in 1990. Competition involves a relay race in which several teams compete against each other and the clock. Equipment includes hurdles, a flyball box, backstop board, and balls.

Obedience

Obedience competitions test owner and dog's ability to work together as a team. There are three types of obedience tests, which include the Limited Obedience Show, Open Obedience Show, and Championship Obedience Show. Competition becomes successively more difficult with each type of show.

Rally Obedience

Rally obedience, or Rally-O, is one of the newest of the canine competitive sports, and it draws on aspects of competitive obedience and agility. The handler and dog execute a course consisting of stations at which they must demonstrate specific skills, which become more difficult at higher levels of competition.

At the Novice level in AKC rally, all exercises are performed on leash. The Novice course includes 10 to 15 stations and no more than 5 stationary exercises. To earn the Rally Novice (RN) title, the dog must earn qualifying scores at three trials. He may then move up to the Rally Advanced class, in which all exercises are performed off leash and include 12 to 17 stations, no more than 7 stationary exercises, and 1 jump (broad jump, high jump, or bar jump). When the dog has earned three qualifying scores in Rally Advanced classes, he may move on to Rally Excellent, in which all exercises except the Honor Exercise are performed off leash. A Rally Excellent course must include 15 to 20 stations, no more than 7 stationary exercises, and 2 jumps. The dog must also perform an on-leash Honor Exercise, remaining in a sit

Rally-O competition and titles have been available from the Association of Pet Dog Trainers (APDT) since 2001. In January 2005, the AKC began to offer competition and titles in rally obedience.

or down at the judge's direction while another dog performs the entire course. To complete the Rally Excellent (RE) title, the dog must earn three qualifying scores.

After a dog earns the RE title, he may continue to strive for the Rally Advanced Excellent (RAE) title, for which he must qualify in both the Rally Advanced B Class and the Rally Excellent B Class at ten trials.

Agility

Agility has become an extremely popular sport for dogs, handlers, and spectators alike over the past 20 years. The breed standard describes the Boxer as "active and agile," making him a great candidate for agility, a sport in which the dog must negotiate a course of jumps, tunnels, and other obstacles. Several organizations sponsor agility competition at novice through advanced levels. The rules, procedures, obstacles, and jump heights differ from one organization to another, so be sure to read the appropriate rule book before entering your dog in competition.

The AKC offers titles for Novice Agility (NA), Open Agility (OA), Agility Excellent (AX), and Master Agility Excellent (MX). The UKC agility program offers titles at four levels of competence, beginning with the U-AGI (Agility I) and progressing to the U-AGII (Agility II), U-ACH (Agility Champion), and U-ACHX (Agility Champion Excellent Title).

Other organizations that exist strictly for agility include the United States Dog Agility Association (USDAA) and the North American Dog Agility Council (NADAC).

Tracking

What could be more natural for a dog than following his nose? This is one sport in which your dog already knows how, and your job is to teach him which track to follow and then to learn to trust him while he works. You need to be reasonably fit to follow your dog's nose through hill and dale, and tracking training requires a considerable amount of time, but training your dog to follow a specific scent trail really is great fun. You can even earn tracking titles if you like.

AKC tracking tests demonstrate your dog's ability to recognize and follow human scent. In order to enter a tracking test, you must first get written certification from an

Your Boxer's nose could lead him to a tracking title.

AKC tracking judge stating that your dog has passed a certification test within the twelve months prior to the date of the tracking test. The certification test should simulate the conditions of an actual TD test. To earn the title Tracking Dog (TD), your dog must pass a tracking test. He can then proceed to the Tracking Dog Excellent Tracking Test to earn the title Tracking Dog Excellent (TDX), or a Variable Surface Tracking Test to earn the Variable Surface Tracking (VST) title. If your dog earns all three titles, he will be a Champion Tracker (CT). Your Boxer can also participate in the ASCA tracking program and earn the ASCA TD and TDX.

Weight Pulling

The United Kennel Club offers weight pull competitions that test a dog's strength and stamina. Although Boxers are not true pulling dogs, some do enjoy pulling in harness and do earn weight pulling titles. To earn titles, a dog must pull a sled or cart holding a specified amount of weight a prescribed distance within a set time limit.

The following titles are awarded for excellence in weight pulling:

• UWP—United Weight Puller

- UWPCH—United Weight Pull Champion
- UWPCHX—United Weight Pull Champion Excellent
- UWPCHV—United Weight Pull Champion Versatile
- UWPCHO—United Weight Pull Champion Outstanding
- UWPCHS—United Weight Pull Champion Supreme

Flyball

No other sport quite compares in raw canine excitement to flyball, which was invented in California in the late 1970s. Dogs love flyball, a sport in which they run relay races as four-dog teams.

In competition, each team member races over a series of four hurdles, hits a peddle to release a tennis ball, snatches the ball in the air, and races back over the hurdles to the starting line. The first team to have all four dogs run without errors wins the heat. Individual dogs earn points toward flyball titles based on the team's time. Your Boxer can earn the titles Flyball Dog (FD), Flyball Dog Excellent (FDX), Flyball Dog Champion (FDCh), Flyball Master (FM), Flyball Master Excellent (FMX), Flyball Master Champion (FMCh), and Flyball Grand Champion (FGDCh). The North American Flyball Association (NAFA) governs flyball competition in North America.

Flying Disc

Ever throw a flying disc for your Boxer to catch or chase? For some people, doggy disc sports are more than a backyard pastime, and the athleticism and energy level of the Boxer make him a natural in this sport.

The International Disc Dog Handlers' Association (IDDHA) sanctions canine disc events, including a test program and a titling program, throughout the world. Before you can compete for titles, you and your dog must demonstrate basic teamwork by successfully completing the test program. Then you may compete for titles, including the BDD (Basic Disc Dog), ADD (Advanced Disc Dog), MDD (Master Disc Dog), CSF (Combined Skills Freestyle title), and DDX (Disc Dog Expert).

Skyhoundz, a separate organization, offers competition in two divisions, Sport and Open. In Open, teams compete for invitations to the World Championships.

The athleticism and energy level of the Boxer make him a natural at canine disc sports.

Dancing With Dogs

Canine musical freestyle is a relatively new competitive sport that combines obedience and dance to display teamwork and rapport between dog and handler. Routines are set to music, and the handler interprets the music with body, arm, and leg motions while the dog performs various movements. The handlers and many of the dogs wear costumes. The emphasis in competition is on teamwork between the handler and the dog, both of whom are judged.

The World Canine Freestyle Organization (WCFO) offers titles in three divisions. Singles Division (one dog and one handler) competitors can earn the titles W-FD (Freestyle Dog), W-FDX (Freestyle Dog Excellent), W-FDM (Freestyle Dog Master), and W-Ch.FD (Champion Freestyle Dog). Pairs Division (two dogs and two handlers) participants can earn the W-PFD, W-PFDX, W-PFDM, and

W-PchFD, with "P" indicating "pairs." Team competitors (multiple dogs, each with a handler) can earn the titles W-TD, W-FDX, W-TFDM, and W-TCh.FD.

Musical Canine Sports International (SCSI) offers titles in Individual (one handler, one dog), Brace, (two handlers, two dogs), and Team (three or more handlers, each with a dog) classes with On-leash and Off-leash divisions at three levels. Dogs can earn the titles of MFD (Musical Freestyle Dog), MFX (Musical Freestyle Excellent), and MFM (Musical Freestyle Master) based on qualifying scores in each of the different classes. You may begin in any class and division but must qualify from the Off-leash Division to enter Masters.

Conformation Shows

If you're like many dog lovers, you've watched Westminster, Crufts, and other dog shows on television. These are conformation shows in which the dog is judged against his breed standard to see how well he conforms to that measure of excellence. The traditional purpose of the show ring was to evaluate the quality of potential breeding stock, so altered animals compete only in special circumstances.

At most shows, judging begins at the class level with those animals who have not yet earned a championship. Dogs (males) are judged against dogs, and bitches (females) against bitches. The classes are organized according to age (6 to 9 Months, 9 to 12 Months, 12 to 18 Months), breeding (Bred By Exhibitor, American Bred), and other factors. The individuals deemed best in each sex at this level are the Winners' Dog (WD) and Winners' Bitch (WB), and they earn points toward their championships.

After the WD and WB are named, the specials—dogs and bitches who already have their championships—enter the ring along with the WD and WB. The judge selects an individual as Best of Breed (BOB), and another as Best of Opposite Sex (BOS), meaning the best individual of the opposite sex to the BOB. In other words, if the BOB is a bitch, the BOS will be a dog, and vice versa. The judge also chooses a Best of Winners (BOW), either the WD or WB.

The Best of Breed continues to the Group competition, where the BOB from each breed is judged against his or her

Whatever sport you may decide to pursue with your dog, please remember why you got a dog in the first place. Winning is exhilarating, but the real treasure to be found in dog sports is the time you and your dog spend enjoying one another's company, win or lose.

Conformation shows judge dogs on how well they fit the breed standard.

own breed standard. Boxers are in the Working Group. At this level of competition, the dog needs to be not only a good representative of his breed standard, but also a true show dog, with the extra sparkle that makes judges take notice. The top four animals in each group are named, and the Group Winners go on to compete for Best in Show.

To enter a dog show, your dog must be registered with the organization that sanctions the show. The largest show sanctioning organization in the US is the AKC. To become an AKC champion (CH), a dog must earn 15 points under three different judges, including two major wins (a win of 3, 4, or 5 points) under two different judges. The number of points your dog earns at a show depends on the number of dogs competing. The rules and procedures for earning championships are quite different in the different registries, so be sure to obtain the rule books, and if possible, observe a show or two before entering.

Deciding to Show Your Boxer

If you don't own a Boxer yet and you think you'd like to try showing in conformation, explain your desire to breeders. Most breeders won't entrust a truly outstanding

pup to a beginner, but many breeders will sell you a good-quality dog with the potential to finish the championship. You can learn the ropes from that dog and find out if you like showing. Because responsible breeders are cautious about where their unaltered pups go, you may be required to keep the breeder's name on the dog's registration papers as co-owner for a while, and there may be other strings attached as well, most often requirements for showing and health screening prior to breeding.

If you already have a Boxer whom you bought as a pet but now you'd like to show, you should be sure your dog conforms to the breed standard. A dog can be a topnotch companion and cute as the dickens and still not be show quality, so try not to let your emotions keep you from looking honestly at your dog's faults as closely as his virtues. Remember that every show dog has faults or traits that could be better, but when an individual has a lot of faults, or a single serious or disqualifying fault, he won't be competitive.

If possible, have someone who knows the Boxer well—a breeder or show judge if possible—evaluate your dog and go over the evaluation with you. Most breeders want only their best pups to represent them in the show ring, so your dog's own breeder may be a good choice if she's involved in showing. Sometimes breeders place show-quality dogs as pets because they consider a good home more important than titles, but often puppies placed as pets have faults that make them noncompetitive. If your dog's breeder doesn't think the dog is show quality, please honor her opinion. Remember, her name is on the dog as his breeder, and he reflects on both her breeding program and her judgment. Enjoy your dog, gain experience in other dog sports, and if you still want to show in conformation, buy a show prospect.

Boxers compete against other Boxers for the "Best of Breed" title.

Tips on Showing Your Boxer

If your Boxer measures up as a show prospect, you both need to start learning the ropes. Showing a dog in conformation is harder than it looks! Go to shows and watch the handlers, noting how the good ones make their dogs stand out in the ring. Find out about handling classes in your area, and consider taking a weekend seminar or two; local clubs often offer classes and sponsor seminars by professional handlers. You also need to learn to groom your Boxer properly for the show ring. He won't need the intensive grooming of some breeds, but you might be surprised at how much does go into presenting a Boxer properly. Read books and magazine and web articles on show handling. If possible, tag along to a few shows with an experienced exhibitor or your dog's breeder. A good mentor is invaluable!

When you're ready to give it a try, start with a small show or a "puppy match." Despite the name, puppy matches are open to adult dogs who don't have major points toward their championships. If your dog wins at a match, he won't earn points toward his title, but the two of you can get used to the ring environment and procedures without the pressures of a real show.

Remember that a dog show is a *show*, and your presentation of yourself and your dog both help create an impression. In a perfect world, dogs would be judged strictly on their merits as representatives of their breeds, but the truth is that the "whole package"—your Boxer's grooming, your appearance, your dog's performance as he moves, stands, and is examined, and your handling ability—all contribute to your success in the show ring. You don't have to dress formally (although if you make it to the Group level in a big show, you should!), but do dress for the occasion. Men conventionally wear dress pants, shirt and tie, and a jacket in conformation. Women can wear pants or a skirt with a nice shirt, sweater, or jacket, or a dress. Wear safe, comfortable shoes that suit the rest of your outfit. Avoid things that flop, like jewelry, scarves, billowy skirts. Solid colors or reasonably subdued patterns work best. Take a look at yourself in a mirror, preferably alongside your dog, before you hit the ring. Remember, you want people to focus on your four-footed companion, not on your fashion sense or *faux pas*. Besides, you want to look good in the photo you have taken with the judge after you win!

If you decide to compete with your Boxer or participate in noncompetitive activities and training, you'll find they are wonderful ways to grow closer to your dog, have fun, get some exercise, learn new things, and spend time with like-minded people. Unfortunately, you'll also run into people who seem to have forgotten what brought them to dog sports in the first place—love for a dog. Winning is wonderful, but not at the cost of sportsmanship and good dog owning skills. Success with dogs isn't just about winning. As a wise obedience judge once told me, "A successful trial is one that you leave with a happy dog."

HEALTH

O F   Y O U R   B O X E R

The Boxer is for the most part a healthy, hardy breed, but like all animals, he can become ill or injured. Some genetic health problems are passed from parent to puppy; other health problems are acquired from the environment. A few health problems may require both a genetic predisposition for the problem and an environmental incident that brings it on.

This chapter begins by looking at some of the steps you can take to keep your Boxer healthy through good veterinary and home care. Then, I'll discuss some of the major problems seen in Boxers. Don't let the information scare you, though—most Boxers are healthy animals.

ROUTINE VETERINARY CARE

Finding the Right Vet

You should feel confident and comfortable with your veterinarian. After all, she's as important to your dog's well-being as your own physician is to yours. Before you bring your new puppy or dog home, take a little time to find the right clinic and individual veterinarian with whom you can enjoy a long-term partnership for your dog's health care.

If you're working with a local breeder or rescue program, ask them as well as your obedience instructor, members of local dog clubs, and friends who have dogs—especially Boxers—what vets they use and what they like and don't like about their vets. If you're new to the area and have no one to ask, look for local veterinarians in the telephone book or on the Internet, and then check out your choices.

Ask for a clinic tour and meet the vet you're considering before you need an appointment. If you're interested in alternative therapies, are opposed to annual vaccinations, or prefer natural diets, ask how the vet feels about such nontraditional approaches to canine health care. It's worth the cost of an office call to be sure you're comfortable putting your dog's health care in the hands of this person, and many vets won't charge anything for a visit of this type.

As in all fields of work, there are competent, caring veterinarians, and there are other vets we'd like to bite. Don't settle for a vet you don't like or trust.

Your Boxer's First Exam

Within the first two to three days after you bring your new puppy or dog home, take him in for a checkup. Your vet will check your Boxer's general health and condition and establish baselines for future reference. She'll examine your dog's skin and coat, ears, gums, bite, and external eye area, as well as listen to his heart and lungs. She should also manipulate his joints to check for range of motion and any signs of discomfort. Take a fecal sample to be checked for internal parasites—many otherwise healthy puppies have roundworms. In addition, be sure to provide a record of vaccinations your puppy or dog has had. There's no point restarting the vaccination series if your pup has already had some or all of his shots.

The first visit is, of course, just the beginning. Good veterinary care will help your Boxer live a long, healthy life.

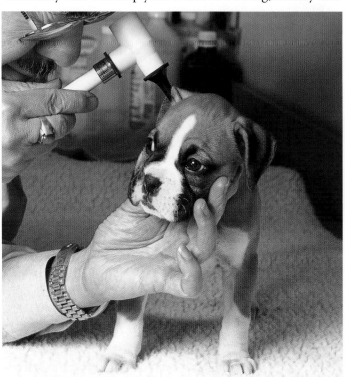

Your veterinarian will check your puppy's ears for signs of infection.

Vaccinations

Dogs, like people, are most vulnerable to infectious diseases during the first months of life. Newborn puppies born to a healthy, properly vaccinated bitch receive some immunity from colostrum, an antibody-rich substance produced by the dam's breasts during the first few days after birth. However, the protection given by colostrum is temporary, and sometime between the fifth and tenth weeks, the pups again become vulnerable to disease. That's why puppies need to be vaccinated.

The traditional approach to puppy vaccinations involves a series of vaccinations beginning at 5 to 8 weeks of age and ending at about 16 weeks, followed by annual boosters. Some vets say those initial vaccines are effective for the life of the dog, while others recommend booster vaccinations one year after the puppy series and every three years from then on. (The exception is rabies vaccinations, which must be given according to state laws.) Other vets prefer to stagger the booster shots so that each is given about every three years, but only one or two are given each year. Some vets recommend checking immunity levels annually with antibody titers, which are blood tests to check for immunity levels. Other vets don't believe that titers are reliable. And of course, many veterinarians and breeders still vaccinate according to traditional protocols. Your best bet is to educate yourself and speak to your vet about what vaccines your dog needs and when. If you're really uncomfortable with one vet's approach, find another vet.

Most vaccines are injected subcutaneously (under the skin) or intramuscularly (into the muscle), but a few are given in nasal sprays. Dogs are commonly vaccinated against some or all of the following diseases.

Rabies

Rabies is caused by a virus that attacks the central nervous system. There are two forms: furious rabies and dumb rabies. Most people picture the furious form in which the animal foams at the mouth and becomes insanely aggressive. Dumb rabies, although less dramatic, is equally deadly. Its victims are paralyzed, and the paralysis begins at the lower jaw and progresses to the limbs and vital organs. Once rabies symptoms appear, the disease is always fatal.

Rabies is transmitted in the saliva of infected animals, usually by way of a bite, and can attack any warm-blooded animal. Rabies is widespread in North America and some other areas of the world. Wild animals, including skunks, foxes, raccoons, coyotes, and bats, commonly transmit the disease to domestic animals, which is why state laws throughout the continental United States require that dogs and cats be vaccinated against rabies annually in some states and every three years in others. Your puppy should have his first rabies vaccination at approximately four months of age, and then receive boosters as required. Rabies does not exist in some island states and nations (Hawaii, Great Britain, and Australia are notable), which is why they maintain strict quarantines on animals coming from areas where rabies occurs.

Distemper

Canine distemper is a highly contagious viral disease that causes respiratory problems, vomiting, and diarrhea. It may also affect the nervous system. Because there are no effective antiviral drugs for canine distemper, the best that can be done for a dog with the disease is to treat the symptoms. The distemper virus damages the linings of the lungs and intestines, so

Be sure to talk to your veterinarian about a vaccination schedule for your puppy.

antibiotics are usually given to fight off bacteria that might attack the damaged organs. Other medications are given to protect the intestines and treat diarrhea, while electrolyte fluids are administered intravenously to prevent dehydration. Vitamins and other essential nutrients are often dispensed by injection to keep up the dog's strength while he is unable to eat normally. Most puppies and about half of adult dogs who contract distemper die of the disease. Dogs who survive are often partly or completely paralyzed and may lose some or all of their vision, hearing, and sense of smell. Puppies normally receive a series of three or four vaccinations against distemper.

Hepatitis

Infectious canine hepatitis is caused by a virus that is spread in the urine of infected dogs. Although the disease can attack many tissues, the liver is usually the most seriously affected.

Mild cases of hepatitis usually run their course in a week or two, during which time the dog will likely be depressed, lose his appetite, and have a slightly elevated temperature. Sometimes the cornea of the eye will turn bluish a week or two after onset of the disease. Coughing, discharge from the nose and eyes, and respiratory problems occur in some dogs, making the disease easy to mistake for bordetellosis (kennel cough). In puppies and some older dogs, the disease can be much more serious, causing abdominal pain, diarrhea, vomiting, edema (swelling from fluid in the tissues), and sometimes jaundice. Severe cases are often fatal.

Treatment for infectious canine hepatitis usually involves antibiotics to prevent secondary infections as the virus weakens the body. Intravenous fluids are often given to prevent dehydration. Puppies are normally given a series of three shots to protect against this disease.

Parvovirus

Canine parvovirus (CPV), or "parvo," is a viral disease that strikes fear in the hearts of dog breeders and puppy owners alike. The virus that causes the disease is passed in the feces of infected dogs and is easily transported from place to place on shoes, paws, and clothing. It survives most disinfectants and extreme temperatures, so once parvo occurs in an environment, it remains a threat for a long time.

Parvo attacks the intestinal tract, heart muscle, and white blood cells, causing vomiting, severe and distinctively foul-smelling diarrhea, depression, high fever, and loss of appetite. Treatment is intensive and expensive, as hospitalization and close monitoring are required. Fluids are given intravenously to prevent dehydration, and drugs are given to control diarrhea and vomiting. Antibiotics are also administered to prevent secondary infections, and additional therapies may be recommended depending on the particular case.

Many dogs die within two to three days of showing initial symptoms. Puppies less than twelve weeks old who contract parvo and survive (with intensive care) often suffer permanent heart damage from myocarditis (inflammation of the heart). Puppies are given a series of three parvo vaccinations to protect against the disease.

Bordetellosis (Kennel Cough)

Canine bordetellosis (bordetella) is a bacterial disease of the respiratory tract that causes a horrendous cough and sometimes copious nasal discharge. Kennel cough usually isn't very serious in an otherwise healthy adult, but it can kill a puppy or elderly dog. Nasal spray vaccinations are usually used to protect against the disease, although injectable vaccines are also available. Antibiotics are sometimes given to dogs with kennel cough, but the disease usually runs its course in a few days in healthy dogs.

Parainfluenza

Canine parainfluenza is a viral infection of the respiratory tract. The primary symptom is a cough (which may be labeled "kennel cough") that becomes more severe after the dog has exercised or is excited. In an otherwise healthy adult dog, the disease usually runs its course in five to ten days, but it can weaken the immune system enough to let secondary bacterial infections take hold. This is why antibiotics are sometimes given. Puppies usually receive a series of three vaccinations, often in combination with other vaccines, to protect against the disease.

Leptospirosis

Canine leptospirosis, or "lepto," is a bacterial disease that attacks the kidneys and/or liver. It is spread in the urine of infected animals. Symptoms include vomiting, convulsions, vision problems, depression, loss of appetite, and fever. Leptospirosis is rare in most areas, although its occurrence may be increasing in some. Treatment includes antibiotics.

The disease appears in several different strains, and unfortunately, the vaccine has little effect on the most common strain. Serious reactions to the vaccine are not uncommon, so many vets and owners elect not to vaccinate against lepto. If a vaccination for lepto seems appropriate given your circumstances, consider having the lepto vaccine given at a different time from the others, and remain at the clinic for half an hour or so after the shot is given in case of a negative reaction.

Coronavirus

Coronavirus is a viral disease that attacks the lining of the small intestine. It occurs in some areas of the United States but not in others. Early symptoms include depression, loss of appetite, and lethargy followed by vomiting (sometimes with blood in the vomit) and projectile diarrhea that is yellowish in color and often contains blood and mucus. Treatment for coronavirus is mostly supportive, and it includes replacing fluids lost through vomiting and diarrhea.

Lyme Disease

Lyme disease is a bacterial disease that occurs only in certain areas of the US. It is spread by the bite of an infected tick, most commonly the tiny deer tick, and causes pain in multiple joints due to arthritic changes. Early symptoms, which typically appear about two months after exposure, may include lethargy, loss of appetite, and fever, followed by lameness. Treatment usually includes antibiotics and analgesics (pain-relieving agents) for the arthritis. Prognosis for recovery depends on how severe the case is and how soon it is diagnosed.

Annual checkups with your Boxer's vet will help keep him in the best of health.

TO BREED OR NOT TO BREED YOUR BOXER

Boxer puppies are darn cute, and you may be tempted to breed a litter. It would be fun, you think. You might make a little money, and perhaps you have friends and relatives who say they want puppies. So why not? The truth is that there are good reasons to breed dogs, and there are even more good reasons not to. Let's look at some of the realities of breeding, as well as the advantages of altering your pet so that you can make an intelligent choice.

The Realities of Dog Breeding

There are already more than enough pet dogs in the world, and all too many of them come from poorly planned litters. The only good reason to breed dogs in this day and age is to produce puppies who combine the very best traits of their breeds and who have as few of the negative traits as possible. Good intentions and love aren't enough; breeding healthy dogs with proper temperaments also requires knowledge, careful planning, time, and money.

As we've seen in this chapter, puppies inherit good and bad traits from their parents. Responsible breeders use science and careful pedigree research to minimize the chances that their puppies will inherit undesirable traits. Screening tests for genetic disease are expensive, and research is time-consuming, but without these tools, the odds increase that your dog will have puppies with serious problems. Besides, if you want responsible, well-informed people to buy your puppies, you will have to show them that you've been responsible as well.

Before she's bred, a Boxer bitch needs at minimum to have her hips x-rayed when she's two years old or older for hip dysplasia, have her heart checked by a canine cardiologist, and have a full thyroid screening panel. You will also want to research the history of these diseases as well as epilepsy and cancer in her close relatives, because she may carry the genes for a disease that she herself doesn't have.

You will also want someone who really knows Boxers to evaluate your bitch in terms of the breed standard, including both her physical traits and her temperament. Don't rely on your veterinarian to do this (unless she's an expert on Boxers); many vets don't know much about good breeding practices or about individual breeds. Keep an open mind

The correct name for a canine female is "bitch," while the term "dog" denotes a male. A young female, then, is a "puppy bitch" and a young male is a "puppy dog." The "dam"(not dame!) is the mother, and the "sire" (not sir!) is the father.

about faults this person points out in your bitch. Knowing what traits in your bitch need improvement will help you select a sire who is strong where she is weak so that the puppies will (hopefully) be better than both parents. If your bitch has a serious fault or one that would disqualify her from the show ring, or if she doesn't pass the health screening tests, then breeding her is almost guaranteed to produce puppies with problems. Even if your puppies will be pets, you'll want them to be good-looking, healthy Boxers their owners can live with and be proud of. All of these requirements apply if you own a male Boxer and want to stand him at stud, of course.

Pregnancy and Whelping

If your bitch is suitable for breeding, you must be able to commit to seeing her through nearly nine weeks of pregnancy and at least another seven weeks of caring for a litter of puppies. Puppies need a safe environment, room to romp, toys, food beginning in about their fourth week, veterinary care, and many hours of gentle handling and socialization. You'll need plenty of cleaning supplies, too—puppies eliminate, throw up, spill food and water, tear and break things, and dig holes. They can sometimes become injured or sick and may need special veterinary care. This is if all goes normally.

Canine pregnancies don't always go according to plan. Pregnancy can bring on gestational diabetes, which can threaten the lives of both the mother and the pups. Puppies can die in utero, causing life-threatening infection in the bitch. Sometimes whole litters are lost well into the pregnancy. Puppies often arrive in the middle of the night or other inconvenient times, and delivery can take a long, long time.

Puppies can be born with many of the same birth defects as human babies, including cleft palates that prevent them from nursing properly, deformed or missing organs, and hydrocephalus. Can you handle the birth of a puppy with serious congenital problems? Can you deal with holding a dying puppy who fades away despite your best efforts to help him live? These are some of the hazards on the breeder's path, and for many people they overshadow the pleasures of breeding dogs.

The decision to breed your Boxer should not be taken lightly—breeding takes time, money, and careful planning.

Of course, pregnancy and whelping aren't the end of the story. Remember all those friends and relatives who wanted puppies? They have a funny way of changing their minds. If you don't find proper homes for your puppies, you remain responsible for them. You should also be willing to take care of the puppies for as long as necessary, as well as take back any pups whose new homes don't work out.

Fortunately, there are excellent breeders who are dedicated to producing fine Boxers despite the risks and responsibilities. On the other hand, far too many people breed their pets without considering the whole picture. Sometimes the pups they produce are fine, but the odds are not in their favor, and when things go wrong, it's the puppies and their buyers who suffer most. Responsible dog breeding is physically and mentally exhausting, expensive, time consuming, and at times, tragic.

Neutering (Spaying and Castrating)

The American Boxer Club (ABC) encourages owners to spay or neuter all but the very best Boxers in terms of breed type, temperament, and individual and inherited health. The AKC, various local and national humane groups, and informed dog trainers, rescuers, veterinarians, and owners agree. The most frequently cited reason for urging owners to spay or neuter pets is pet overpopulation. Visit your local animal shelter, or call a Boxer rescue organization, and you'll get some idea of the number of Boxers who lose their homes each year. Responsible dog ownership involves a lot more than providing food, shelter, veterinary care, training, exercise, and love for a pet. It also involves a commitment to the welfare of any puppies your pet produces. The harsh truth is that most animals in shelters—including cute little puppies—are never adopted. Your Boxer shouldn't give birth to or sire a single puppy whom you would not be willing to care for throughout his life if necessary.

As important as it is, population control isn't the only reason to spay or neuter your Boxer. Spaying (removal of the ovaries and uterus) eliminates the dangers of pregnancy and whelping, and if it's done before your puppy bitch has her first heat, spaying prevents life-threatening cancers or infections of the uterus and ovaries and greatly reduces your pet's risk of developing mammary tumors as she ages. A spayed bitch is also easier to live with than an intact bitch, and she won't attract lovelorn doggy boys to your doorstep.

What about the old idea that having a litter will calm your bitch down? Not true. Training, proper exercise, and maturity lead to calmer behavior, not motherhood. Some people also think that having a litter will make a bitch more sweet and loving. On the contrary, the responsibilities of motherhood are likely to focus your pet's attention away from her human family, and she may become very protective of her puppies. Even without pups, many unspayed bitches are moody and more aggressive, especially with other bitches, because of fluctuating hormone levels. Spaying will make your female pet much more stable emotionally.

Castration benefits male dogs in similar ways. It will keep your dog from siring puppies, with or without your permission, and will minimize some stud-dog behaviors that people find annoying, including territorial urine marking and roaming in search of females. When an unneutered male dog detects a bitch in heat, which he can do from miles away, he stops eating, whines, paces, howls, slobbers, and becomes very pushy and distracted. Neutering will not turn your male dog into a wimp, but it will probably make him more tolerant of other male dogs and less likely to pick fights. Castration will also prevent testicular cancer and reduces your dog's chances of developing prostate problems.

Will spaying or neutering change your Boxer's basic personality? No. In fact, by eliminating the urges brought on by sex hormones, neutering will allow the positive aspects of your pet's personality to shine. Neutering your pet will not make him overweight, either. Obesity develops when a dog eats too much food and gets too little exercise or has another health problem, such as hypothyroidism. Unless your Boxer is an outstanding example of the breed, there's just no good reason not to have him or her neutered.

Spaying and neutering can help keep your Boxer healthy.

PARASITES

Like all animals, your Boxer is a potential host for a wide range of parasites that live in or on his body. Some parasites do no harm to their hosts, but others cause direct damage or carry disease or both. Fortunately, modern science has found ways to prevent or control most common parasites of dogs.

External Parasites

External parasites, including fleas, ticks, and mites, are more than just disgusting and annoying—they also carry disease, and their bites can become infected or cause allergic reactions in some dogs. The more you know about these little monsters, the better you'll be able to protect your dog (and yourself) from them.

Fleas

Fleas are small insects with hard shells of red, black, or brown. Adult fleas suck blood from their hosts, and flea larvae eat the adults' blood-rich feces, or "flea dirt, which looks like tiny clusters of blackish specks on an animal's skin. You can identify flea dirt by wetting it slightly—flea dirt will turn red because it's mostly comprised of blood.

Fleas usually lay their eggs in grass, carpets, rugs, bedding, and on the host animal. The eggs normally hatch in 4 to 21 days, depending on the environmental temperature. The larvae, which look like tiny maggots, molt twice and then form a pupa and metamorphose into adult fleas. Flea pupae can survive long periods until temperature or vibration from a nearby host stimulates the adult fleas to emerge.

Fleas are more than annoying little pests. They carry disease and tapeworm larvae from host to host. When they infest a host in large numbers, they can consume enough blood to cause anemia, and a dog who is allergic to flea saliva may scratch himself raw from even a single flea bite, opening the way to infection. Fleas also bite people. If you find fleas on your dog or in your house or yard, you will need to treat all your pets as well as their environment. Over-the-counter flea controls are not the most effective (or cost efficient) treatments, and they can even be dangerous, so talk to your vet about the best flea-control options for your situation.

Check your Boxer for external parasites after he's been outside.

Ticks

Ticks are small arthropods (relatives of spiders). They have eight legs and are usually round and flat unless they are engorged with blood from the host or gravid with eggs, in which case they look like beans with legs. Your Boxer may pick up ticks in tall grass, brush, or wooded areas, and animals and birds can carry ticks into your yard and home. If ticks are a problem where you live, talk to your vet about a prevention program.

When a tick eats, it buries its head in the host's flesh and gorges on blood. Like fleas, ticks carry diseases, including Rocky Mountain spotted fever and ehrlichiosis, so it's important not to squeeze fluid from the tick into the host, which can transmit disease, or pull the tick's head off in the host's skin, which can cause an infection. A fine-toothed flea comb works well for detecting ticks.

To remove a tick safely, dab it with a strong saline solution, iodine, or alcohol to make it loosen its grip, and then gently pull it straight out using forceps, tweezers, or your fingers with a tissue over the tick. Check the skin—you should see a small hole where the tick bit your dog. A black spot means you have left the head. In either case, clean the site with alcohol or an antibacterial cleanser, dry, and apply antiseptic ointment. Wash your hands and the instrument you used to remove the tick. Check the spot daily for signs of infection, particularly if the head was left behind. In most cases the site will heal quickly, but if you see any swelling or redness after 24 hours, talk to your vet.

The tiny little deer tick is a particular threat in some areas because it spreads Lyme disease, which can cripple a dog (or a person). Deer ticks are so small they are often not noticeable until after they're been feeding on the host for several days, and by then they've probably done their damage. Ask your veterinarian about the danger of Lyme disease where you live, and ask her whether you should vaccinate your Boxer. If you walk in areas where ticks hide out, check your dog carefully afterward—ticks don't usually attach to the host for several hours, so you may be able to catch them before they chow down.

Mites

Mites are microscopic arachnids that can cause a variety of diseases in dogs. One such disease, mange, is caused by any of several species of tiny mites that eat skin debris, hair follicles, and tissue. Dogs with mange typically suffer hair loss, crusty patches of irritated skin, and severe itching. They often scratch themselves raw, providing easy entry for viral, fungal, or parasitic infections. Some forms of mange are contagious; others are not. If you think your dog might have mange, don't try home remedies—they probably won't be effective and may make matters worse. Your veterinarian can examine the mites under a microscope, determine the species that is attacking your dog, and then prescribe an appropriate treatment program. She can also tell you how to keep other pets safe from infection.

Internal Parasites

Several species of worms live as parasites in dogs and other animals. Although some of them have virtually no effect on the host animal's health, others can cause illness, and in large enough numbers, even death. Evidence of most internal parasites can be found by microscopic examination of the host's feces, so your puppy should have fecal exams when he receives his vaccinations. Adult dogs should also have fecal exams at least once a year. If you see signs of worms in your dog's stools or around his anus, take a specimen to your vet. Again, don't rely on over-the-counter or home remedies—different worms respond to difference treatments, so it's essential to know what type of parasite you're trying to eliminate.

Heartworm

Heartworms are caused by a parasitic worm that infests the host's heart, eventually clogging the vessels and causing congestive heart failure. Heartworm disease is spread by mosquitoes. When a mosquito bites a dog infected with heartworms, it ingests the larvae and subsequently transmits the larvae when it bites another dog. The microscopic larvae travel through the arteries to the host's heart, where they mature and reproduce.

Heartworm disease causes no symptoms until a large number of worms infest the heart. At that advanced stage of the disease, the dog will have symptoms of congestive heart failure: coughing (especially after exercise), difficulty breathing, and low energy levels. His coat will become dull, and his abdomen may become enlarged. By the time the disease has advanced that far, it may be too late for effective treatment, so prevention is essential

Heartworm disease is a problem in some places and practically nonexistent in others. Ask your vet about the risk of heartworm disease where you live and travel with your dog. Fortunately, heartworm disease is easy to prevent with a variety of medications, although it's important to realize that even the best prevention is not one hundred percent effective. All dogs should be checked every year or two for heartworm, as early diagnosis and treatment are essential. If you live in an area where heartworm is a problem, your Boxer should be kept on a heartworm prevention program throughout his life.

If you notice your Boxer scratching more than usual, you should check with your veterinarian.

Ringworm

Ringworm is caused by a fungus, not a worm. It usually causes raw-looking bald circles, but sometimes bald patches appear without the rawness. Like many fungal infections, ringworm is difficult to treat effectively. It is also highly contagious, spreading easily to other animals and to people. If you find any sort of bald spot on your dog, take him to the vet for proper diagnosis and treatment, and ask your vet how to prevent spread of the disease. Don't wait to see if it gets better or fool around with home remedies—you may end up with a much bigger problem.

Roundworm

Roundworms, which look like strings of spaghetti up to 8 inches (20 cm) in length, are very common. Even puppies from responsible breeders with clean facilities and healthy dogs often have roundworms because if the mother has had roundworms at any time in her life, she can pass them to her puppies before or after they're born. Testing the mother for roundworms before breeding or whelping won't reveal roundworm larvae that are encysted in her muscle tissue or mammary glands, and nursing puppies can ingest roundworm larvae in their mother's milk. Puppies may also pick up the parasites by ingesting roundworm eggs, which can be passed on by a wide variety of other animals, including earthworms, cockroaches, rodents, poultry, and other dogs.

A large or chronic infection will cause the puppy to develop a potbelly, have diarrhea, and vomit. At first he'll seem to be hungry all the time, because the roundworms eat the food digesting in the pup's intestines. Eventually, the puppy will become so malnourished and weak that he will stop eating. Fortunately, roundworms are easy to eliminate with the proper medication. Human beings can get roundworms, too, so practice careful hygiene until your vet declares your puppy free of worms, and teach your children to do the same.

Tapeworm

Tapeworms require two different hosts during their life cycle. Tapeworm larvae inhabit intermediate hosts such as a mice, rabbits, and fleas. If your dog ingests such an infected animal, the larvae then develop into adult tapeworms in your dog's intestines, where they eat digesting food and grow up to several feet in length. Tapeworms often do not show up in fecal specimens and are diagnosed instead when rice-like segments break off of the worm and stick to the tissue and hair around the dog's anus. If you see signs of tapeworm on your dog, talk to your vet—a special wormer is required to kill tapeworm. If your Boxer kills and eats wild animals or has had a case of fleas, be especially alert for tapeworm evidence.

Other Internal Parasites

Other internal parasites, including hookworms, whipworms, threadworms, coccidia, and giardia, can also infect puppies and dogs, causing weight loss, anemia, respiratory infection, and diarrhea. The best way to protect your dog from the damage caused by parasites is to keep his environment clean, be observant, and have him examined regularly by a vet.

Exercise for the Life of Your Boxer

Boxers are energetic dogs who need adequate exercise to be at their best physically, mentally, and emotionally. This is especially true through adolescence and young adulthood. On the other hand, your puppy's bones will still be growing until he is about a year old (at which time the growth plates close), so some cautions are in order when exercising young Boxers.

Growth plates (also called epiphyseal plates or the epiphysis) are soft areas of immature bone found near the ends of the puppy's leg bones. Growth—mainly lengthening—of the bones comes from the growth plates. The soft growth plates in young dogs are vulnerable to fractures and other injuries, and as long as they are open, you need to monitor the type of exercise your Boxer engages in and discourage high-impact and leg-twisting activities such as jumping, leaping after flying disks, and so forth. Around one year of age, calcium and minerals harden the soft area in a process usually referred to as the closing of the growth plates. Most growth comes to an end at this time.

As your Boxer ages, he will probably lose that adolescent rowdiness he once had, but he still needs to exercise to remain physically, mentally, and emotionally healthy. Obesity is all too common in adult Boxers, and lack of sufficient exercise is a major contributor to life-shortening excess weight. Coupled with a proper diet, exercise appropriate to your dog's general health and condition will help keep his weight down, his cardiovascular and digestive systems healthy, and his muscles toned. Exercise will also make your dog happier and alleviate boredom, and walks and games of fetch will keep the bond between the two of you strong.

If your Boxer is over seven and has not been exercising regularly, take him to your vet for a checkup and geriatric screening before beginning an exercise program.

Coughing during or after exercise should be reported to your veterinarian—it can be a sign of heart trouble. If your dog seems to have trouble catching his breath after moderate exercise, again, check with your vet. If your Boxer has orthopedic problems such as hip or elbow dysplasia or has arthritis, speak to your vet about appropriate exercise. On-leash walking is easier on the joints than running and can be broken into two or three shorter walks during the day rather than one long one.

HEALTH ISSUES IN BOXERS

All breeds of dogs (and all crosses between different breeds or mixed breeds) are potentially subject to inherited health problems. Most Boxers are healthy, but it pays to be aware. The following are descriptions of some common health problems that afflict Boxers.

Aortic Stenosis

Aortic stenosis (AS), one of the most common heart defects observed in Boxers and other dogs, refers to

Exercise will help alleviate boredom in your high-energy Boxer.

narrowing caused by a ring of fibrous tissue beneath the aortic valve. The job of the left ventricle of the heart is to pump oxygenated blood through the aortic valve and into the aorta, from which it then flows throughout the body before returning to the lungs for reoxygenation. Stenosis causes the left ventricle to work harder to force blood through the abnormally small opening, leading to hypertrophy (thickening) of the left heart muscle and dilation (ballooning) of the aorta due to the increased pressure. The flow of blood is reduced, and many dogs with this disease faint or even die suddenly, especially after exercise. Some dogs show no symptoms prior to sudden death.

Aortic stenosis is known to be inherited, but the mode of transmission has not yet been identified.

Your regular veterinarian may pick up a heart murmur or hear a swishing sound caused by abnormal blood flow through the valve during a routine examination. Murmurs often accompany aortic stenosis, but not all heart murmurs indicate disease, especially in young animals. If you want to test your Boxer for AS, your best resource is a veterinary cardiologist. An Echo/Doppler test (echocardiogram) can be performed when your dog is at least a year old or even earlier if he shows signs of heart disease. Although a useful tool, the test isn't foolproof—false results, both negative and positive, sometimes occur, especially when the stenosis is slight and symptoms subtle. The skill of the technician operating the equipment may also be a factor, so if possible, choose a clinic that performs lots of echocardiograms and whose clinicians have been trained according to standards set by the American College of Veterinary Internal Medicine for cardiology specialists.

If your Boxer is diagnosed with AS, you may be able to lengthen his life by controlling his weight and restricting his exercise to a moderate level, especially in hot weather. Some veterinarians also prescribe beta blockers to help the dog's heart function better.

Bloat

Bloat is the term commonly used to refer to the life-threatening condition called "gastric dilatation and volvulus" (GDV). When a dog bloats, his stomach fills with air and may rotate on itself, cutting off the flow of blood and causing the stomach tissue to die. Symptoms of bloat include restlessness, unwillingness to lie down, abdominal swelling, rapid, shallow breathing, dry heaving, retching, and heavy salivation. Bloat may cause the dog to go into shock as well.

If you suspect your dog may be bloating, get him to a veterinarian *immediately*. Even with proper treatment, about a third of dogs who bloat don't survive.

You can reduce your Boxer's risk of bloat by keeping him at a reasonable weight and by feeding him two or three meals a day rather than one. If he gulps his food, find a way to slow his eating. (See Chapter 4 for some ideas).

Boxer Cardiomyopathy

One of the most devastating health issues in Boxers is Boxer cardiomyopathy (BCM), a heart condition that usually shows no symptoms until the affected dog collapses. Most Boxers do not recover from their first and only BCM attack.

BCM is believed to be an inherited condition that affects about half of all Boxers. It causes arrhythmia (abnormal rhythms) of the ventricles, which do the bulk of the heart's job of pumping blood. The most common arrhythmia in

BCM is premature ventricular contraction (PVC), a condition in which the ventricle contracts earlier than it should. If single PVCs occur only once in a while, the dog will probably show no signs of heart disease, but if a number of them occur together, the heart will be unable to contract properly. Blood flow to the brain and other organs will then stop, and the dog will collapse. A series of PVCs can cause the heart to stop (cardiac arrest), and the dog will die. In a few cases, the heart swells, leading to congestive heart failure, which typically causes lethargy, breathing difficulty, coughing, and abdominal swelling.

BCM is extremely difficult to diagnose before symptoms appear. A conventional electrocardiogram (ECG), which measures electrical activity in the heart at rest, will not detect the sporadic arrhythmias typical of Boxer cardiomyopathy. Similarly, a standard echocardiogram (an ultrasound of the heart) will not detect the infrequent arrhythmias typical of BCM. The most effective current diagnostic tool for detecting BCM is a portable ECG called a Holter monitor. The Boxer wears the device for 24 hours, and the heart's activity is measured during normal activities. The results usually indicate the individual Boxer's risk of BCM.

The rare Boxer who survives an episode of BCM is usually treated with medications designed to help the heart maintain a normal rhythm. A complete cardiac workup and careful monitoring are also essential to prevent another attack. Research is underway at The Ohio State University to determine how BCM is inherited and to see how diet, exercise, PCV occurrence, and heart rate affect the risk of collapse or heart failure in affected dogs.

Brachycephalic Syndrome

Brachycephalic syndrome is a combination of disorders of the upper airway seen individually or in combination in brachycephalic, or "short-headed," breeds, including the Boxer. The disorders that compose the syndrome include:

- stenotic nares—abnormally narrow nostrils.
- elongated soft palate—tissue of the soft palate, which separates the nasal passage from the oral cavity, extends loosely into the throat; although this rarely causes respiratory distress in Boxers, it can cause the dog to snort.

The Boxer's short muzzle makes him susceptible to heatstroke, which is why it's so important to keep him cool on warm days.

- tracheal stenosis—abnormal narrowing of the trachea (windpipe), which can make anesthesia extremely dangerous.

The disorders associated with brachycephalic syndrome reduce the ability of the dog to cool himself effectively by panting, making him much more susceptible to heatstroke than a dog with a longer muzzle.

Common symptoms of brachycephalic syndrome, which usually appears when the dog is between one and four years of age, include noisy breathing, heat or exercise intolerance, gagging, and occasionally vomiting. In severe cases, the dog may pass out.

Treatment depends on the severity of the condition but may include restricted exercise, anti-inflammatory medications, and in severe cases, surgery.

Cancer

Cancers of various kinds affect all dogs, including the Boxer. Some cancers progress very slowly, others very quickly, and they can attack any part of the body. Treatment options for dogs with cancer are very similar to those available for people: surgery, radiation, and chemotherapy. Early diagnosis greatly improves the chances for successful treatment. Let's look at some of the most common cancers in dogs.

Brain Tumors

Boxers, like other brachycephalic (short-nosed) breeds, are more susceptible than other dogs to a type of brain tumor known as a glioma, which begins in the glial cells (supporting cells) of the brain. These tumors range from slow-growing, relatively benign tumors to highly aggressive glioblastoma multiform tumors that compress and kill off surrounding brain tissue as they grow. Unfortunately, these highly malignant tumors are resistant to treatments currently available. Brain tumors usually attack older dogs.

Symptoms depend on the size and location of the tumor. A tumor in the front of the brain may cause behavioral changes, seizures, walking in circles, and lack of coordination. If it occurs in the brain stem, a tumor may cause nystagmus (rapid, involuntary eye movements), head tilting, staggering, and difficulty swallowing. Your regular veterinarian may make an initial diagnosis of a brain tumor but will likely recommend that your dog see a veterinary neurologist for further testing. Diagnostic tests that may be recommended could include a CT ("CAT") scan, MRI, CT-guided biopsy, or surgical biopsy.

Treatment options will depend on the location and size of the tumor. If your dog is suffering from seizures, your vet may prescribe an antiseizure drug. Surgery to remove part or all of the tumor may be a possibility if it is accessible, but surgical treatment for glioma usually involves the risk of damaging surrounding brain tissue. Radiation is commonly used to reduce the size and slow the growth of the tumor, but the individual dog's response to radiation therapy is highly variable. Chemotherapy is used less often and is less effective.

The tests and treatments for brain tumors carry a high price, both financially and emotionally for you and physically for your dog. Your veterinarian can present options, but in the end it will be your sad responsibility to weigh your dog's age, chances for recovery, and other factors as you decide what option is appropriate for you and your dog.

Lymphosarcoma

Lymphosarcoma is a common, very aggressive cancer of lymphocytes, the cells that stimulate the body's immune response. Lymphosarcoma can affect the dog's lymph nodes, liver, spleen, and other organs, typically in middle-aged or older dogs. Diagnosis is usually made after unidentified lumps or swellings are examined. If the cancer is found early enough, chemotherapy may add months or even years to the dog's life.

Osteosarcoma

Osteosarcoma is an aggressive cancer of the bone, and it is highly metastatic, or prone to spreading to other parts of the body. Treatment usually involves amputation of the affected limb followed by chemotherapy. Because of the aggressive nature of the disease and the rapid changes in cancer treatments, a dog with osteosarcoma should in most cases be treated by a veterinary oncologist. Success of treatment varies depending on how far the cancer has spread, but with proper care, some dogs live at least a year after treatment.

Mammary Tumors

Mammary tumors may be small, benign growths in the breast tissue or large, aggressively metastatic cancers. This is the most common type of tumor in unspayed bitches (female dogs), and it usually appears when the bitch is between five and ten years old, although tumors sometimes affect younger bitches. This is also one of the most easily preventable canine cancers; a bitch who is spayed before coming into her first heat has very little chance of developing mammary cancer. The risk is a bit higher if she's spayed after her first heat but before she's two-and-a-half years old, and higher yet for bitches spayed later in life or never spayed.

Mammary tumors occasionally develop in male dogs. When they do, the tumors are usually aggressive and the prognosis is poor. If they are detected early, mammary tumors in bitches can often be treated successfully, so if you feel any sort of growth in or around your dog's breasts, see your vet. Treatment may involve surgery, chemotherapy, and radiation therapy.

Testicular Tumors

Testicular tumors are among the most common tumors in older intact (unneutered) male dogs. Testicular tumors are reasonably easy to diagnose, and surgical castration is usually all the treatment required, although more aggressive therapy may be necessary in some cases. The risk of testicular cancer is much higher in dogs who have one or both testicles undescended into the scrotum, so neutering of any dog with retained testicles is essential for his health.

Canine Hip Dysplasia (CHD)

Canine hip dysplasia, or CHD, is a serious, potentially crippling condition in which the bones that make up the hip joint are malformed and do not fit together properly. This poor fit makes the dog prone to the development of painful arthritis. CHD is inherited, and it cannot be diagnosed or ruled out just by watching a dog move. The Orthopedic Foundation for Animals (OFA) reports that approximately 11 percent of the nearly 3,400 Boxers tested have been found to have some degree of hip dysplasia. It is vital that all Boxers used for breeding be x-rayed and that the x-rays be evaluated by the Orthopedic Foundation for Animals or PennHIP in the United States, or the appropriate equivalent program elsewhere. Some dogs with CHD never show clinical symptoms, but these animals should not be used for breeding.

Not all dogs with hip dysplasia have obvious symptoms, but many show varying degrees of lameness and pain. Some have a bunny-hop gait, and some have trouble getting up and don't want to jump or stand on their hind legs. Treatment depends on the severity of the condition in the individual dog. Treatment may involve some combination of pain medications, nutritional support, weight control, limited exercise, physical therapy, or surgery. Definitive diagnosis of HD requires x-rays of the hips.

Deafness in White Boxers

White markings on Boxers are caused by a gene that is expressed differently in different individuals. In about 75 percent of Boxers who have white markings, the white is confined to the face, chest, belly, and legs. The rest of the time, though, the white extends farther. Most white Boxers are as healthy as their colored brethren, but if the white (which is essentially lack of pigment) affects the ears, the dog may be partially or completely deaf. A dog with bilateral deafness is deaf in both ears and has no hearing whatsoever.

A dog with unilateral deafness (sometimes called a "uni") is deaf in one ear.

It takes a dedicated person with outstanding dog training skills and a safe environment to raise and train a totally deaf dog. Compassion is not enough; good intentions can lead to disaster if not supported by the skills, knowledge, and environment needed to manage a dog who can't hear. If you are up to the task, some excellent books and Internet

Occasionally, white Boxers may experience hearing problems.

resources do offer support and information for owners of deaf dogs.

A Boxer with unilateral deafness can function normally as a pet, but owners need to be aware that the dog may have some relatively minor problems, such as initial difficulty locating the source of a sound. It's important to understand, too, that it's not always easy to determine deafness, especially unilateral deafness, because dogs respond to many stimuli. The Brainstem Auditory Evoked Response (BAER) test is used to determine partial or complete deafness in dogs. The test measures the brain's response to clicking sounds in each ear, and puppies can be tested any time after five weeks of age. Responsible breeders test all dogs prior to breeding them, and they test all puppies before they go to their new

Acepromazine Sensitivity

Acepromazine is a tranquilizer that is commonly prescribed by veterinarians for a variety of purposes. Unfortunately, it can be lethal for Boxers or part-Boxers, as it can cause potentially fatal heart arrhythmia, profound hypotension (life-threatening low blood pressure), profound bradycardia (slow heart rate), and respiratory arrest. As a precaution, have your veterinarian place a warning against use of acepromazine prominently on the outside and inside of your Boxer's health record, and if your dog requires anesthesia for any reason, remind your vet that acepromazine should not be used. For your dog's sake, don't assume that your vet knows about this problem in Boxers.

homes. Dogs who are deaf, or who produce deaf puppies, should not be used for further breeding.

Ear Infections

Otitis externa, or inflammation of the outer ear canal, is very common in dogs. Signs of infection or other problems in the ear include strong odor, rubbing or scratching of the ears and head, shaking or tilting the head, discharge from the ear, swelling or redness, and tenderness around the ears. Many factors can contribute to ear infections, and to be effective, the treatment must be right for the individual case. Consequently, if your Boxer shows signs of ear problems, see your vet. Don't apply ear cleaners or medications without consulting your vet, because the wrong treatment can cause more damage and pain. To keep your Boxer's ears healthy, check them once a week and keep them clean. (For more information, see Chapter 5.)

Causes of Ear Disease

The following are some common causes of ear disease:
- Allergies, such as atopy or food allergies
- Parasites
- Foreign bodies, e.g., plant awns
- Trauma
- Hormonal abnormalities
- Hereditary or immune conditions
- Tumors
- Allergies
- Parasites
- Bacteria and Yeast
- Foreign Bodies
- Trauma (including self-inflicted trauma from scratching)

Seizures and Epilepsy

Seizures, sometimes called "fits," can have any of several causes. Many seizures are the result of nonhereditary, environmental causes, including physical trauma to the head, chemicals, medications, disease, and heatstroke, among others. If a dog suffers seizures due to environmental influences such as drugs or chemicals, removing the cause will usually stop them. If head trauma is the cause, antiseizure medication may control the seizures so that the dog can live a reasonably normal life.

Epilepsy is a seizure disorder that occurs in most breeds of dogs and in mixed breeds. Although the term "epilepsy" is sometimes applied to any dog with seizures, true, or primary (also known as idiopathic), epilepsy is inherited. (Secondary epilepsy, in contrast, refers to a seizure condition with a known cause.) Epilepsy cannot be cured, but it can often be controlled with medication. Most epileptic dogs can live fairly normal lives, but under no circumstances should a dog with epilepsy be bred. Before you buy a Boxer puppy, ask the breeder about epilepsy in the dog's bloodlines. One relative with seizures is not necessarily cause for concern, but beware if there are multiple close relatives with the disease.

Thyroid Disease

Many breeds of dogs are genetically predisposed to hypothyroidism ("low" or underactive thyroid). The OFA reports that almost 15 percent of Boxers tested under their thyroid protocols have tested abnormal. Symptoms of low thyroid include lack of energy, weight gain, coarse coat, loss of hair, infertility or inability to carry fetuses to term, and in some cases, neurological problems. Once diagnosed, hypothyroidism is treated with a daily dose of thyroxine, a synthetic thyroid hormone.

The basic thyroid screening test (called T4) that is often used isn't very accurate—it can give both false positives and false negatives. More accurate results can be obtained from a panel of tests. Not all diagnostic laboratories are equipped to run these tests, but your vet can send samples to any of several labs around the country for analysis. Hypothyroidism can often be diagnosed by the tests before clinical symptoms appear, so testing every so often isn't a bad idea, especially because thyroid disease can develop slowly. Treatment usually consists of a daily oral dose of synthetic thyroxine, which must be continued for the rest of the dog's life. Boxers used for breeding should be tested every year or so, and affected dogs should not be bred.

Urinary Incontinence

Urinary incontinence commonly occurs in middle-aged Boxers who are neutered. Females are affected more frequently than males, although the problem can affect both sexes. Typically, the dog "leaks" while sleeping, or occasionally while awake, especially when getting up from a prone position. Don't let the risk of future incontinence scare you out of altering your dog, though—incontinence is almost always an easy problem to treat, and it is far less serious than unwanted puppies, uterine or testicular cancer, and other potential problems present in sexually intact dogs.

Before beginning treatment for incontinence, it's important to rule out serious problems, including urinary tract infection (UTI), kidney disease, diabetes mellitus, Cushing's disease, or hypercalcemia. Your vet will palpate your dog's bladder when it's full and after urination, observe your dog urinating, and have a urinalysis performed. She will also consider your dog's complete medical history, including reproductive status (intact or altered), age at altering, previous UTIs, description of incontinence problem and age at onset, and history of disease or trauma. Drug treatment for simple "leaking" is straightforward, comparatively inexpensive, and highly effective.

Learning canine first aid will help keep everyone calm in case of emergency.

EMERGENCIES

Emergencies can happen in a heartbeat, and smart as he is, your Boxer can't assemble the basic first-aid supplies and critical information that might save his life in an emergency. As always, he's relying on you!

Canine First Aid

Knowing how to respond if your Boxer needs emergency care will make you breathe easier. Consider adding a good veterinary first-aid book to your home library, or take a pet first-aid or cardiopulmonary resuscitation (CPR) class offered by a continuing education program, veterinary school, vet clinic, or the Red Cross. In an emergency, provide first aid, then get your dog to a veterinarian as quickly as possible. Call ahead so they know you're on your way, and drive carefully.

Common Canine Emergencies

Poisons

Poisons are all around our homes, and despite our best efforts to protect them, our dogs are sometimes exposed to

First-Aid Kit for Dogs

You can purchase a canine first-aid kit from many pet supply stores or veterinarians, or you can put one together yourself. Here are the basics of a good doggy first-aid kit:

- A muzzle to keep your dog from biting when frightened or in pain;
- Hydrogen peroxide in 3% solution (USP). Write the purchase date on the bottle, and replace with a fresh bottle once a year;
- Bulb syringe or medicine syringe;
- Saline eye solution to flush eyes;
- Artificial tear gel to lubricate eyes after flushing;
- Antidiarrheal (ask your vet's advice);
- Topical antibiotic;
- Mild grease-cutting dishwashing liquid to remove skin contaminants;
- Rubber gloves for handling contaminated dog;
- Forceps or tweezers;
- Good basic veterinary first-aid manual;
- Small notebook and pen or pencil for taking notes (for instance, time poison was ingested, time of a seizure, intervals between seizures, bowel movements, vomiting, etc.);
- Telephone numbers for your veterinarian, closest emergency veterinary facility, National Animal Poison Control Center (NAPCC)—1-888-4ANI-HELP or 1-900-443-0000—and a friend or neighbor who could help in an emergency.

them. Prescription and nonprescription medications can be deadly, especially in larger-than-normal amounts or when taken together. Chocolate, raisins, or grapes can kill a dog. More than 700 types of plants, many of them found in our gardens and homes, contain toxins, as do fertilizers, herbicides, and insecticides. Poisons designed to attract pests, like slug bait, ant poisons, and mouse or rat poisons, will attract your dog, and a dog can even be poisoned by eating a poisoned animal. Puppies and dogs who swallow lead paint chips or dust, toys, drapery weights, fishing weights, lead shot, some types of tiles and insulation, and improperly glazed ceramic bowls, or who drink water that's passed through lead pipes, may suffer from lead poisoning. Antifreeze is another poison that, while sweet and attractive to pets, is lethal. Some spider bites are poisonous, and dogs can even be allergic to bee stings. It's a toxic world out there!

Symptoms of poisoning may include vomiting; diarrhea; loss of appetite; swelling of the tongue and other mouth tissues, face, or body; excessive salivation; and staggering, seizures, or collapse. If you know or suspect that your dog has been exposed to poison, contact your veterinarian, emergency clinic, or animal poison center immediately. Don't assume that your dog is safe if you don't see symptoms—some symptoms are slow to appear, and

delaying treatment could make the difference between life and death.

Broken Bones

Broken bones or fractures are not uncommon in active dogs. If you think your dog has a fracture, keep him quiet so that he doesn't cause more damage to the bone or surrounding tissue, nerves, and blood vessels. If he will lie quietly, place him on a blanket or board so that you can carry him without disturbing the injury. Fractures of bones in the head, neck, and body can be life threatening, so it's important to prevent movement. Don't assume that if your dog walks on a leg it's not broken. My own dog, Rowdy, walked on a broken leg. If you have not had first-aid training, don't try to apply a splint, as you could cause more damage. Keep the dog quiet, carry him to a vehicle, and get him to a veterinarian. Have someone else drive if possible so you can keep your dog calm and quiet.

Treatment of a fracture will depend on the location and severity of the fracture and the dog's age, but veterinary care is essential for all fractures to control pain and prevent more damage.

Cuts, Bleeding, and Bites

Cuts, bleeding, and bites are also not uncommon injuries for an active Boxer. If your pet experiences one of these wounds, first evaluate the injury. Some areas, such as the nose and tongue, bleed profusely even from tiny cuts, while some serious injuries barely bleed at all. If the injury is minor, clean it gently with hydrogen peroxide, and apply pressure with a clean towel or gauze pad until the bleeding slows or stops. Apply a topical antibiotic ointment, and watch the area for a few days for signs of infection. If the wound is bleeding and is deep or long, apply pressure with a clean towel, cloth, or gauze pad, and get your dog to your veterinarian as soon as possible. Your Boxer may need stitches and other treatment.

If your dog is bitten by another animal, clean the wound, stop the bleeding if necessary, and call your vet. Bite wounds are always at high risk of infection because the mouth contains enormous populations of bacteria. Bites may also introduce disease, including rabies. Many bites do not bleed, which may seem like a good thing, but punctures that don't bleed trap bacteria and can develop serious infections. Even if the wound doesn't require immediate veterinary care, your vet will probably prescribe an oral antibiotic.

Heatstroke

Heatstroke (hyperthermia) is a potentially lethal condition that occurs when an animal's body temperature rises beyond a safe range. Dogs don't sweat, and they can't cool themselves as efficiently as humans can. Brachycephalic (short-faced) breeds like the Boxer are even more susceptible to overheating than are their longer-muzzled cousins. Never leave your dog in a vehicle on a warm day, even for a few minutes. In hot weather, don't leave him outside without shade (especially on concrete or asphalt), and restrict his exercise in very hot weather. Make sure he always has access to clean, cool water, and if he has trouble breathing, a history of heatstroke, or is elderly or ill, keep him indoors and cool when it's hot outside. Symptoms of heatstroke include red or pale gums; bright red tongue; sticky, thick saliva; rapid panting; and vomiting and/or diarrhea. The dog may act dizzy or weak, and he may go into shock.

A dog with moderate heatstroke (body temperature from 104°F to 106°F) will probably recover if given first aid immediately. Use a hose, shower, or tub of cool, not icy, water to wet and cool him, and check his temperature every ten minutes. Continue the cooling process until his temperature is down to 103°F. Give him a rehydration fluid or water, and take him to the veterinarian.

Severe heatstroke (body temperature over 106°F) can kill your dog or cause permanent organ damage. Immediate veterinary treatment is essential. If you're more than five minutes from the vet and your dog is conscious, follow the cooling procedures outlined above until his temperature is down to 106°F. Then, wrap him in a cool, wet towel or blanket and proceed to the vet. Your veterinarian will continue cooling your dog if necessary, as well as monitor his temperature and check for shock, breathing problems, kidney failure, and other potential complications. The vet will also administer fluids to your dog to help stabilize his temperature, and she will advise you about follow-up care.

Once a dog has had heatstroke, he's more susceptible to a recurrence, so be especially careful not to put him in risky situations.

Frostbite

Frostbite is uncommon in dogs, but it can affect your Boxer if he's outdoors in severely cold weather for too long. Frostbite refers to the formation of ice crystals in body tissues, most commonly the ear tips, toes, and tail. The ice crystals restrict the flow of blood in the injured area, and without treatment, gangrene (tissue death) can set in. Frostbite is often hard to detect on a dog, but signs include redness of the skin initially, with a shift to white or gray. The first thing to do if you suspect your Boxer is frostbitten is to get him to a warmer place. Then, apply warm (about 102°F) compresses to the affected areas, or immerse the area in warm water. When the area feels warm, gently pat it dry— *do not rub*. Keep your dog warm, and get him to a veterinarian as soon as possible.

Preparing for Disasters

No one can help your dog in an emergency if they don't know he's there. Labels on the front and back doors can be used to let neighbors and emergency personnel know that your dog is in the house. Note his favorite hiding place if he has one, as well as where they can find his leash, his collar if he doesn't routinely wear it, and the name and telephone number of your vet and a reliable friend to call if you aren't available. A crate kept within easy reach will provide a familiar, safe means of transporting your dog in case of evacuation.

It's a good idea to sign a boarding and medical care authorization form so that someone else can leave your dog in a safe place if necessary. File one copy with your veterinarian, keep one in your car, and give copies to one or two trusted neighbors or friends. If your area is prone to natural disasters, make arrangements with a veterinarian and a boarding kennel an hour or so away in case your own vet is affected by the emergency. Most shelters for people do not accept pets.

A doggy evacuation kit may be useful, too. Pack supplies in a waterproof container, and keep it where you can reach it easily. Pack two days' worth of dry dog food in sealed bags

Keep your Boxer's safety in mind, and you'll have a loving family pet for years to come.

or containers, one or two bottles of water, and a week's supply of your dog's medications (replace once a month to keep them fresh) and first-aid supplies. If your dog takes medication that requires refrigeration, note that on top of the evacuation kit. Tuck in an envelope with enough cash or travelers checks to get you through at least two days. Finally, keep copies of the following documents in your animal evacuation kit, and leave copies with a friend or relative in case the kit becomes lost.

- Veterinary and vaccination records.
- Information about any medical condition your dog has and necessary treatment or medication.
- Proof of ownership. Include copies of your dog's registration certificate, adoption papers, proof of purchase (contract or receipt), license tag number, and microchip or tattoo number.
- A data sheet including your dog's name, breed, color, sex, size, and age. Attach a recent color photo of your dog; if he becomes lost and you can't get to your home, the photo may be useful for making flyers.
- Important telephone numbers (keep copies in your vehicles and with friends and neighbors), including your

If Your Boxer Becomes Lost

Having your Boxer become lost is terrible, but it sometimes happens despite your best precautions. You can increase your chances of bringing him home by following a few simple steps.

- *Provide your Boxer with identification* by attaching a name tag, registration tag, and rabies tag attached to your dog's collar so that anyone who finds him can also find you. Make sure the information is current. Consider having your dog tattooed or microchipped as well for permanent identification—collars and tags can get lost or be removed. Permanent ID, in addition to a good photograph of your dog, also give you proof of ownership if that is ever disputed.
- *Act fast*, because the more quickly you begin a serious search, the more likely that you'll find your dog.
- *Advertise* in your local newspaper, and consider running ads in newspapers from neighboring towns as well. A Boxer can travel a long way in a short time.
- *Call all shelters and veterinarians* in your own county and adjacent counties, and contact your closest Boxer rescue organization. Keep in mind that shelter staff could overlook your dog or fail to recognize your dog as a Boxer, so visit shelters yourself as often as possible.
- *Use the Internet* to post information about your dog on Boxer discussion lists, and ask that the information be forwarded to other appropriate lists.
- *Post flyers* with a color photo of your dog, information on where and when he was lost, and your telephone number.
- *Ask neighborhood children* if they've seen your Boxer. They are more likely than adults to notice a dog in the area. Ask area schools for permission to hang your poster where students will see it.

numbers away from home (work, cell phone, pager); friend or relative to contact if you aren't available; your veterinarian; a local boarding kennel; a veterinarian or boarding kennel 25 to 50 miles away that can board your dog if necessary; local animal shelter and animal control; local health department, Red Cross chapter; and other emergency response agencies.

ALTERNATIVE APPROACHES TO CANINE HEALTH CARE

Over the past several decades, many people have become interested in nonconventional approaches to animal as well as human health. The terms alternative, complementary, or holistic medicine are used to refer to practices that include formal disciplines such as chiropractic, acupuncture, homeopathy, herbal therapy, and nutrition, and other practices such as massage therapy, shiatsu, reiki, TTouch, and others. The common thread that ties all of these approaches together is the belief that physical and emotional factors work together to create health or illness.

The following are some brief descriptions of just a few of the many alternative approaches to canine health care that are available.

If you want to explore some alternative approaches to your Boxer's health, do your research and consult with your veterinarian.

Homeopathy

Homeopathic medicine treats symptoms of illness with minute, diluted amounts of substances that, in larger doses, would cause those same symptoms. The goal is to stimulate the body to respond by curing itself. Most homeopathic substances come from plants, although some are from animal and mineral sources. Homeopathic treatments are said by some people to be effective in treating diseases, allergies, injuries, and poisons, but some of the substances used can be toxic in the wrong doses. As a result, it's not a good idea to try homeopathic remedies without consulting a veterinarian who is trained in homeopathic veterinary medicine.

Acupuncture

Acupuncture was developed in ancient China. In modern veterinary usage, needles, massage, heat, and lasers are used to stimulate the release of hormones, endorphins, and other chemical substances that enable the body to fight off pain and disease.

Chiropractic

Chiropractic medicine deals with the relationship between the spinal column and the nervous system, and its effect on overall health. Many competitors find that regular chiropractic adjustments improve their dogs' performances.

Herbal Therapy

Herbal therapy can be highly effective, but herbs should be used with great caution and only under the supervision of someone who is knowledgeable about their properties. Some herbs are highly toxic.

YOUR AGING BOXER

Our dogs don't live nearly long enough, and they enter their senior years far too soon. The age at which any individual dog becomes "elderly" varies, but you may begin to notice age-related changes when your Boxer is between 9 and 12 years old. One of the first signs of age will probably be a general slowing down. Your older dog may become more deliberate about his daily routine and less tolerant of changes, and he may lose some or all of his hearing and vision. He may take on a "bony" feel as he loses muscle and weight, and his movements may become slower and stiffer.

Behavioral changes are very common in elderly dogs. Your senior Boxer may worry about things he barely noticed before. Changes in his environment or normal routine may confuse him, and he may suffer from separation anxiety when you aren't with him. He may also sleep more deeply and longer than he used to and may spend more time just lying around.

Don't assume that your Boxer doesn't want your attention just because he no longer asks you to play as often. He still loves you and needs your attention and affection. Elderly dogs, like elderly people, can become lonely and depressed, so don't forget that snuggles and belly rubs are as important as ever to your dog's emotional well-being. Regular, gentle grooming will stimulate your dog's circulation and help keep his muscles supple, and will also alert you to lumps and bumps that need veterinary attention. Take your Boxer for walks as long as he's up to them—moderate exercise is good for his physical and mental health.

Change is an inevitable part of the aging process, of course, but if you notice a sudden or extreme difference in your Boxer's body or behavior, schedule a visit with the vet. Some medical conditions mimic or exaggerate the effects of aging, and some can be managed with medication or other

Make sure your older Boxer is comfortable and receives plenty of attention.

therapies. Even if he's in good health, your old friend should have regular checkups, and many vets recommend exams every six months for their senior patients. With proper care, your Boxer is likely to live to a ripe old age.

APPENDIX
BREED STANDARDS

THE AMERICAN KENNEL CLUB BREED STANDARD

General Appearance: The *ideal* Boxer is a medium-sized, square-built dog of good substance with short back, strong limbs, and short, tight-fitting coat. His well-developed muscles are clean, hard, and appear smooth under taut skin. His movements denote energy. The gait is firm yet elastic, the stride free and ground-covering, the carriage proud. Developed to serve as guard, working, and companion dog, he combines strength and agility with elegance and style. His expression is alert and his temperament steadfast and tractable.

The chiseled head imparts to the Boxer a unique individual stamp. It must be in correct proportion to the body. The broad, blunt muzzle is the distinctive feature, and great value is placed upon its being of proper form and balance with the skull.

In judging the Boxer first consideration is given to general appearance and overall balance. Special attention is then devoted to the head, after which the individual body components are examined for their correct construction, and the gait evaluated for efficiency.

Size: Adult males 23 to 25 inches; females 21? to 23? inches at the withers. Proper balance and quality in the individual should be of primary importance since there is no size disqualification.

Proportion: The body in profile is square in that a horizontal line from the front of the forechest to the rear projection of the upper thigh should equal the length of a vertical line dropped from the top of the withers to the ground.

Substance: Sturdy, with balanced musculature. Males larger boned than females.

Head: The beauty of the head depends upon the harmonious proportion of muzzle to skull. The blunt muzzle is 1/3 the length of the head from the occiput to the tip of the nose, and 2/3rds the width of the skull. The head should be clean, not showing deep wrinkles (wet). Wrinkles typically appear upon the forehead when ears are erect, and are always present from the lower edge of the stop running downward on both sides of the muzzle.

Expression: Intelligent and alert.

Eyes: Dark brown in color, frontally placed, generous, not too small, too protruding, or too deepset. Their mood-mirroring character, combined with the wrinkling of the forehead, gives the Boxer head its unique quality of expressiveness. Third eyelids preferably have pigmented rims.

Ears: Set at the highest points of the sides of the skull, the ears are customarily cropped, cut rather long and tapering, and raised when alert. If uncropped, the ears should be of moderate size, thin, lying flat and close to the cheeks in repose, but falling forward with a definite crease when alert.

Skull: The top of the skull is slightly arched, not rounded, flat, nor noticeably broad, with the occiput not overly pronounced. The forehead shows a slight indentation between the eyes and forms a distinct stop with the topline of the muzzle. The cheeks should be relatively flat and not bulge (cheekiness), maintaining the clean lines of the skull as they taper into the muzzle in a slight, graceful curve.

Muzzle and Nose: The muzzle, proportionately developed in length, width, and depth, has a shape influenced first through the formation of both jawbones, second through the placement of the teeth, and third through the texture of the lips. The top of the muzzle should not slant down (downfaced), nor should it be concave (dishfaced); however, the tip of the nose should lie slightly higher than the root of the muzzle. The nose should be broad and black.

Bite and Jaw Structure: The Boxer bite is undershot, the lower jaw protruding beyond the upper and curving slightly upward. The incisor teeth of the lower jaw are in a straight line, with the canines preferably up front in the same line to give the jaw the greatest possible width. The upper line of the incisors is slightly convex with the corner upper incisors fitting snugly in back of the lower canine teeth on each side. Neither the teeth nor the tongue should ever show when the mouth is closed.

The upper jaw is broad where attached to the skull and maintains this breadth, except for a very slight tapering to the front. The lips, which complete the formation of the muzzle, should meet evenly in front. The upper lip is thick and padded, filling out the frontal space created by the projection of the lower jaw, and laterally is supported by the canines of the lower jaw. Therefore, these canines must stand far apart and be of good length so that the front surface of the muzzle is broad and squarish and, when viewed from the side, shows moderate layback. The chin should be perceptible from the side as well as from the front. Any suggestion of an overlip obscuring the chin should be penalized.

Neck: Round, of ample length, muscular and clean without excessive hanging skin (dewlap). The neck should have a distinctly arched and elegant nape blending smoothly into the withers.

Back and Topline: The back is short, straight, muscular, firm, and smooth. The topline is slightly sloping when the Boxer is at attention, leveling out when in motion.

Body: The chest is of fair width, and the forechest well-defined and visible from the side. The brisket is deep, reaching down to the elbows; the depth of the body at the lowest point of the brisket equals half the height of the dog at the withers. The ribs, extending far to the rear, are well-arched but not barrel-shaped.

The loins are short and muscular. The lower stomach line is slightly tucked up, blending into a graceful curve to the rear. The croup is slightly sloped, flat and broad. The pelvis is long, and in females especially broad. The tail is set high, docked, and carried upward. An undocked tail should be severely penalized.

Forequarters: The shoulders are long and sloping, close-lying, and not excessively covered with muscle (loaded). The upper arm is long, approaching a right angle to the shoulder blade. The elbows should not press too closely to the chest wall nor stand off visibly from it. The forelegs are long, straight, and firmly muscled, and, when viewed from the front, stand parallel to each other. The pastern is strong and distinct, slightly slanting, but standing almost perpendicular to the ground. The dewclaws may be removed. Feet should be compact, turning neither in nor out, with well-arched toes.

Hindquarters: The hindquarters are strongly muscled, with angulation in balance with that of the forequarters. The thighs are broad and curved, the breech musculature hard and strongly developed. Upper and lower thigh are long. The legs are well-angulated at the stifle, neither too steep nor over-angulated, with clearly defined, well "let down" hock joints. Viewed from behind, the hind legs should be straight, with hock joints leaning neither in nor out. From the side, the leg below the hock (metatarsus) should be almost perpendicular to the ground, with a slight slope to the rear permissible. The metatarsus should be short, clean, and strong. The Boxer has no rear dewclaws.

Coat: Short, shiny, lying smooth and tight to the body.

Color: The colors are fawn and brindle. Fawn shades vary from light tan to mahogany. The brindle ranges from sparse but clearly defined black stripes on a fawn background to such a heavy concentration of black striping that the essential fawn background color barely, although clearly, shows through (which may create the appearance of reverse brindling). White markings, if present, should be of such distribution as to enhance the dog's appearance, but may not exceed one-third of the entire coat. They are not desirable on the flanks or on the back of the torso proper. On the face, white may replace part of the otherwise essential black mask, and may extend in an upward path between the eyes, but it must not be excessive, so as to detract from true Boxer expression. The absence of white markings, the so-called "plain" fawn or brindle, is perfectly acceptable, and should not be penalized in any consideration of color. *Disqualifications* Boxers that are any color other than fawn or brindle. Boxers with a total of white markings exceeding one-third of the entire coat.

Gait: Viewed from the side, proper front and rear angulation is manifested in a smoothly efficient, level-backed, ground covering stride with a powerful drive emanating from a freely operating rear. Although the front legs do not contribute impelling power, adequate reach should be evident to prevent interference, overlap, or sidewinding (crabbing). Viewed from the front, the shoulders should remain trim and the elbows not flare out. The legs are parallel until gaiting narrows the track in proportion to increasing speed, then the legs come in under the body but should never cross. The line from the shoulder down through the leg should remain straight although not necessarily perpendicular to the ground. Viewed from the rear, a Boxer's rump should not roll. The hind feet should dig in and track relatively true with the front. Again, as speed increases, the normally broad rear track will become narrower. The Boxer's gait should always appear smooth and powerful, never stilted or inefficient.

Character and Temperament: These are of paramount importance in the Boxer. Instinctively a hearing guard dog, his bearing is alert, dignified, and self-assured. In the show ring his behavior should exhibit constrained animation. With family and friends, his temperament is fundamentally playful, yet patient and stoical with children. Deliberate and wary with strangers, he will exhibit curiosity, but, most importantly, fearless courage if threatened. However, he responds promptly to friendly overtures honestly rendered. His intelligence, loyal affection, and tractability to discipline make him a highly desirable companion. Any evidence of shyness, or lack of dignity or alertness, should be severely penalized.

The foregoing description is that of the ideal Boxer. Any deviation from the above described dog must be penalized to the extent of the deviation.

Disqualifications: Boxers that are any color other than fawn or brindle. Boxers with a total of white markings exceeding one-third of the entire coat.

Approved February 11, 2005
Effective March 30, 2005

THE KENNEL CLUB BREED STANDARD

General Appearance: Great nobility, smooth-coated, medium-sized, square build, strong bone and evident, well developed muscles.

Characteristics: Lively, strong, loyal to owner and family, but distrustful of strangers. Obedient, friendly at play, but with guarding instinct.

Temperament: Equable, biddable, fearless, self-assured.

Head and Skull: Head imparts its unique individual stamp and is in proportion to body, appearing neither light nor too heavy. Skull lean without exaggerated cheek muscles. Muzzle broad, deep and powerful, never narrow, pointed, short or shallow. Balance of skull and muzzle essential, with muzzle never appearing small, viewed from any angle. Skull cleanly covered, showing no wrinkle, except when alerted. Creases present from root of nose running down sides of muzzle. Dark mask confined to muzzle, distinctly contrasting with colour of head, even when white is present. Lower jaw undershot, curving slightly upward. Upper jaw broad where attached to skull, tapering very slightly to front. Muzzle shape completed by upper lips, thick and well padded, supported by well separated canine teeth of lower jaw. Lower edge of upper lip rests on edge of lower lip, so that chin is clearly perceptible when viewed from front or side. Lower jaw never to obscure front of upper lip, neither should teeth nor tongue be visible when mouth closed. Top of skull slightly arched, not rounded, nor too flat and broad. Occiput not too pronounced. Distinct stop, bridge of nose never forced back into forehead, nor should it be downfaced. Length of muzzle measured from tip of nose to inside corner of eye is one-third length of head measured from tip of nose to occiput. Nose broad, black, slightly turned up, wide nostrils with well defined line between. Tip of nose set slightly higher than root of muzzle. Cheeks powerfully developed, never bulging.

Eyes: Dark brown, forward looking, not too small, protruding or deeply set. Showing lively, intelligent expression. Dark rims with good pigmentation showing no haw.

Ears: Moderate size, thin, set wide apart on highest part of skull lying flat and close to cheek in repose, but falling forward with definite crease when alert.

Mouth: Undershot jaw, canines set wide apart with incisors (six) in straight line in lower jaw. In upper jaw set in line curving slightly forward. Bite powerful and sound, with teeth set in normal arrangement.

Neck: Round, of ample length, strong, muscular, clean cut, no dewlap. Distinctly marked nape and elegant arch down to withers.

Forequarters: Shoulders long and sloping, close lying, not excessively covered with muscle. Upper arm long, making right angle to shoulderblade. Forelegs seen from front, straight, parallel, with strong bone. Elbows not too close or standing too far from chest wall. Forearms perpendicular, long and firmly muscled. Pasterns short, clearly defined, but not distended, slightly slanted.

Body: In profile square, length from forechest to rear of upper thigh equal to height at withers. Chest deep, reaching to elbows. Depth of chest half height at withers. Ribs well arched, not barrel-shaped, extending well to rear. Withers clearly defined. Back short, straight, slightly sloping, broad and strongly muscled. Loin short, well tucked up and taut. Lower abdominal line blends into curve to rear.

Hindquarters: Very strong with muscles hard and standing out noticeably under skin. Thighs broad and curved. Broad croup slightly sloped, with flat, broad arch. Pelvis long and broad. Upper and lower thigh long. Good hind angulation; when standing, the stifle is directly under the hip protuberance. Seen from side, leg from hock joint to foot not quite vertical. Seen from behind, legs straight, hock joints clean, with powerful rear pads.

Feet: Front feet small and cat-like, with well arched toes, and hard pads; hind feet slightly longer.

Tail: Customarily docked.
    Docked: Set on high and carried upward.
    Undocked: Set on high and carried gaily, not curled over back. Of moderate thickness. In overall balance to the rest of dog.

Gait/Movement: Strong, powerful with noble bearing, reaching well forward, and with driving action of hindquarters. In profile, stride free and ground covering.

Coat: Short, glossy, smooth and tight to body.

Colour: Fawn or brindle. White markings acceptable not exceeding one-third of ground colour.
Fawn: Various shades from dark deer red to light fawn.
Brindle: Black stripes on previously described fawn shades, running parallel to ribs all over body. Stripes
contrast distinctly to ground colour, neither too close not too thinly dispersed. Ground colour clear, not
intermingling with stripes.

Size: Height: dogs: 57-63 cms (22 1/2-25 ins); bitches: 53-59 cms (21-23 ins). Weight: dogs: approximately 30-32 kgs (66-70 lbs); bitches: approximately 25-27 kgs (55-60 lbs).

Faults: Any departure from the foregoing points should be considered a fault and the seriousness with which the fault should be regarded should be in exact proportion to its degree and its effect upon the health and welfare of the dog.

Note: Male animals should have two apparently normal testicles fully descended into the scrotum.

July 2001

Conversion Chart

US Units	Multiplied By	Equals Metric Units
Length		
Inches	2.5400	Centimeters
Feet	0.3048	Meters
Yards	0.9144	Meters
Miles	1.6093	Kilometers
Area		
Square inches	6.4516	Square centimeters
Square feet	0.0929	Square meters
Square yards	0.8361	Square meters
Acres	0.4047	Hectares
Volume		
Cubic feet	0.0283	Cubic meters
Cubic yards	0.7646	Cubic meters
Gallons	3.7854	Liters
Weight		
Foot-pounds	1.3830	Newton-meters
Pounds	0.4536	Kilograms

Temperature

Fahrenheit to Celsius: Subtract 32 from the Fahrenheit temperature. Divide the answer by 9, then multiply by 5.

RESOURCES

Organizations

American Boxer Club
Secretary: Sharon Fosseem
E-mail:acbquestions@americanboxerclub.org
http://americanboxerclub.org

American Kennel Club (AKC)
5580 Centerview Drive
Raleigh, NC 27606
Telephone: (919) 233-9767
Fax: (919) 233-3627
E-mail: info@akc.org
www.akc.org

Association of Pet Dog Trainers (APDT)
150 Executive Center Drive Box 35
Greenville, SC 29615
Telephone: (800) PET-DOGS
Fax: (864) 331-0767
E-mail: information@apdt.com
www.apdt.com

Canadian Kennel Club (CKC)
89 Skyway Avenue, Suite 100
Etobicoke, Ontario M9W 6R4
Telephone: (416) 675-5511
Fax: (416) 675-6506
E-mail: information@ckc.ca
www.ckc.ca

Delta Society
875 124th Ave NE, suite 101
Bellevue, WA 98005
Telephone: (425) 226-7357
Fax: (425) 235-1076
E-mail: info@deltasociety.org
www.deltasociety.org

International Agility Link (IAL)
Global Administrator: Steve Drinkwater
85 Blackwall Road
Chuwar, Queensland 4306
Australia
Telephone: (+61) 7 3202 2361
E-mail: yunde@powerup.au
www.agilityclick.com/~ial

North American Flyball Association (NAFA)
1400 West Devon Avenue #512
Chicago, IL 60660
Telephone: (800) 318-6312
Fax: (800) 318-6318
www.flyball.org

The Kennel Club
1 Clarges Street
London
W1J 8AB
Telephone: 0870 606 6750
Fax: 0207 518 1058
www.the-kennel-club.org.uk

United Kennel Club (UKC)
100 E. Kilgore Road
Kalamazoo, MI 49002-5584
Telephone: (269) 343-9020
Fax: (269) 343-7037
E-mail: pbickell@ukcdogs.com
www.ukcdogs.com

Publications

Books

Lane, Dick, and Neil Ewart. *A-Z of Dog Diseases & Health Problems.* New York: Howell Books, 1997.

Rubenstein, Eliza, and Shari Kalina. *The Adoption Option: Choosing and Raising the Shelter Dog for You.* New York: Howell Books, 1996.

Serpell, James. *The Domestic Dog: Its Evolution, Behaviour and Interactions with People.* Cambridge: Cambridge University Press, 1995.

Magazines

AKC Family Dog
American Kennel Club
260 Madison Avenue
New York, NY 10016
Telephone: (800) 490-5675
E-mail: familydog@akc.org
www.akc.org/pubs/familydog

AKC Gazette
American Kennel Club
260 Madison Avenue
New York, NY 10016
Telephone: (800) 533-7323
E-mail: gazette@akc.org
www.akc.org/pubs/gazette

The Boxer Review
E-mail: info@boxerreview.com
www.boxerreview.com

The Boxer Ring
5060 Old Carpenter Road
Edwardsville, IL 62025
Phone: (618) 960-6316
Fax: (618) 659-9000
Email: theboxerring@earthlink.net
www.theboxerring.com

Dog & Kennel
Pet Publishing, Inc.
7-L Dundas Circle
Greensboro, NC 27407
Telephone: (336) 292-4272
Fax: (336) 292-4272
E-mail: info@petpublishing.com
www.dogandkennel.com

Dog Fancy
Subscription Department
P.O. Box 53264
Boulder, CO 80322-3264
Telephone: (800) 365-4421
E-mail: barkback@dogfancy.com
www.dogfancy.com

Dogs Monthly
Ascot House
High Street, Ascot,
Berkshire SL5 7JG
United Kingdom
Telephone: 0870 730 8433
Fax: 0870 730 8431
E-mail: admin@rtc-associates.freeserve.co.uk
www.corsini.co.uk/dogsmonthly

Internet Resources

PRO Boxers

(www.pro-boxers.com)

This website is a primary resource for everything one could possibly want to know about Boxers, with links to clubs and organizations in the US, UK, and Canada, as well as conformation, international rescue services, and agility training sites.

Boxer-Dog.org

(www.boxer-dog.org)

This site lists a plethora of Boxer clubs and rescue organizations in North America and the UK and has compiled an extensive list of breeders and adoption shelters, as well as up-to-date news articles about this breed.

Animal Welfare Groups and Rescue Organizations

American Humane Association (AHA)
63 Inverness Drive East
Englewood, CO 80112
Telephone: (303) 792-9900
Fax: 792-5333
www.americanhumane.org

American Society for the Prevention of Cruelty to Animals (ASPCA)
424 E. 92nd Street
New York, NY 10128-6804
Telephone: (212) 876-7700
www.aspca.org

Boxer Rescue USA
http://www.americanboxerrescue.org/bxrrsq/

Boxer Rescue International
http://www.americanboxerrescue.org/bxrrsq/international.htm

Royal Society for the Prevention of Cruelty to Animals (RSPCA)
Telephone: 0870 3335 999
Fax: 0870 7530 284
www.rspca.org.uk

The Humane Society of the United States (HSUS)
2100 L Street, NW
Washington DC 20037
Telephone: (202) 452-1100
www.hsus.org

Veterinary Resources

Academy of Veterinary Homeopathy (AVH)
P.O. Box 9280
Wilmington, DE 19809
Telephone: (866) 652-1590
Fax: (866) 652-1590
E-mail: office@TheAVH.org
www.theavh.org

American Academy of Veterinary Acupuncture (AAVA)
100 Roscommon Drive, Suite 320
Middletown, CT 06457
Telephone: (860) 635-6300
Fax: (860) 635-6400
E-mail: office@aava.org
www.aava.org

American Animal Hospital Association (AAHA)
P.O. Box 150899
Denver, CO 80215-0899
Telephone: (303) 986-2800
Fax: (303) 986-1700
E-mail: info@aahanet.org
www.aahanet.org/index.cfm

American Holistic Veterinary Medical Association (AHVMA)
2218 Old Emmorton Road
Bel Air, MD 21015
Telephone: (410) 569-0795
Fax: (410) 569-2346
E-mail: office@ahvma.org
www.ahvma.org

American Veterinary Medical Association (AVMA)
1931 North Meacham Road – Suite 100
Schaumburg, IL 60173
Telephone: (847) 925-8070
Fax: (847) 925-1329
E-mail: avmainfo@avma.org
www.avma.org

British Veterinary Association (BVA)
7 Mansfield Street
London
W1G 9NQ
Telephone: 020 7636 6541
Fax: 020 7436 2970
E-mail: bvahq@bva.co.uk
www.bva.co.uk

INDEX